BBC good food eat well

HEALTHY SLOW COOKER RECIPES

BBC good food eat well

HEALTHY SLOW COOKER RECIPES

BBC
BOOKS

10 9 8 7 6 5 4

BBC Books, an imprint of Ebury Publishing
20 Vauxhall Bridge Road,
London SW1V 2SA

BBC Books is part of the Penguin Random House
group of companies whose addresses can be
found at global.penguinrandomhouse.com

Penguin
Random House
UK

Photographs © BBC Magazines 2017
Recipes © BBC Worldwide 2017
Book design © Woodlands Books Ltd 2017
All recipes contained in this book first appeared in
BBC *Good Food* magazine.

First published by BBC Books in 2017

www.eburypublishing.co.uk

A CIP catalogue record for this book is available
from the British Library

ISBN 9781785941986

Printed and bound in Italy by Printer Trento S.r.l.

Typeset in India by Integra Software Services Pvt.
Ltd, Pondicherry

Nutritionist: Kerry Torrens
Cover Design: Interstate Creative Partners Ltd
Production: Alex Merrett
Picture Researcher: Gabby Harrington

Penguin Random House is committed to a
sustainable future for our business, our readers and
our planet. This book is made from Forest
Stewardship Council® certified paper.

BBC Books would like to thank the following people
for providing photos. While every effort has been
made to trace and acknowledge all
photographers, we should like to apologise should
there be any errors or omissions.

Will Heap 19, 41, 99, 121, 123, 155, 225; Jon Whitaker
23, 231; Clare Winfield 25; Mike English 21, 27, 29, 31,
33, 35, 37, 65, 77, 79, 87, 91, 101, 107, 115, 135, 141, 147,
149, 153, 159, 161, 163, 171, 173, 175, 177, 179, 181, 183,
185, 189, 191, 193, 195, 241, 243, 245, 247, 251, 253,
257; Maja Smend 43, 249; Rob Streeter 45, 85, 139,
233, 269; Myles New 47, 55, 111, 113, 169, 205, 275;
Charlie Richards 49; David Munns 51, 81, 131; Philip
Webb 53, 59, 71, 237, 239; Jean Cazals 57; David
Munns 61, 63, 73, 75, 127; Adrian Lawrence 67, 83,
207, 235; Peter Cassidy 69, 143; Gareth Morgans 95,
157; Lis Parsons 97, 125, 129, 145, 187, 281; Roger
Stowell 103; Toby Scott 105, 209; Stuart Ovenden
109, 211, 213, 229, 255, 279; William Lingwood 117;
Francine Lawrence 119; Sam Stowell 133, 137, 203,
223; Angela Nilsen 151; Lara Holmes 271, 273.

All the recipes in this book were created by the
editorial team at Good Food and by regular
contributors to BBC Magazines.

Contents

· ·

Introduction

· ·

Whether you are out all day and want to come back to a hot home-cooked meal, or you like to effortlessly entertain, using a slow cooker is a fantastic and energy-saving way to cook.

Here we have brought together a collection of healthy recipes from some of our previous best-selling books with recipes that have performed well on bbcgoodfood.com that we have adapted and tested for slow cookers, as well as new *Good Food* recipes, to show you how versatile a slow cooker can be.

It can also be an asset in the kitchen to help you part-cook conventional recipes like pies and ragus, make up batches of curry base or even make your morning porridge.

We have included family recipes like healthier chilli con carne, lasagne and shepherd's pie, but also authentic curries and flavour-packed dishes that you can enjoy with friends when you can spend a little more time in the kitchen.

To get the best flavours from the ingredients, we found that it is better for most recipes to pre-fry meat and onions rather than put them in raw, but if you would rather get the recipe ready the night before, just cook from cold and add 1–2 hours to our cooking time to build in the heating process. Check manufacturer's instructions for advice too.

Getting the best from your slow cooker

Every slow cooker is different, so make sure you keep your manufacturer's manual handy when using it. However, here we'll share with you the *Good Food* team's top tips for slow cooking.

- Lots of the recipes can be changed to fit in with your lifestyle, so follow your manual's guidelines on decreasing or increasing cooking times by changing the temperature of the slow cooker. However, we've found rice, pasta and oat-based dishes really work best when cooked on High for the shortest time possible.
- Rinse rice well first. The more starch you can wash off the rice, the better the finished dish.
- Slow cookers vary considerably in size, so we've written a variety of recipes, for a variety of portions. Many of these are easily halved or doubled – check the individual recipes for recommendations.
- If you want to adapt your own recipes to suit a slow cooker, look for something similar in this book and copy the timings – but reduce the liquid in your original recipe. Here are a few points we think may help.

FLAVOUR
- Brown onions before adding them to the recipe as per the original recipe, this adds both colour and flavour.
- Brown all red meat and chicken as per the original recipe if you can, though this is not as essential it will add flavour.
- If the recipe says to brown veggies, again this isn't vital but will add flavour.
- Toast spices in a frying pan to get rid of any raw spice flavour.

- Bring wine to the boil before adding it and bubble it for a while to reduce it or it will taste harsh.

TIMINGS
- You can add cooked pulses at the same time as the meat, slow cookers don't break them down in the same way conventional cooking does, or you can stir them through at the end of cooking and allow them to heat through.
- Add greens at the end, and give them no more than 30 mins cooking.
- Add fresh herbs at the end.
- Allow 8 hours for red meat to tenderise.
- Allow 6 hours for lentils/pulses/veggies dishes.
- Seafood doesn't need long, add it within the last 30 mins.

LIQUID AMOUNTS
- Halve liquid amounts of wine, stock or water, as slow cookers do not evaporate off any liquid.

Be aware of ingredients that will release a lot of water whilst cooking. If they are being used in large quantities, take down the liquid proportions even further to compensate.

THICKENING SAUCES
If the sauce of a stew or a casserole is a little thin for your liking, mix 1 tbsp cornflour to a paste with a splash of the sauce, then transfer to a pan with a ladleful of the sauce and bring to the boil to thicken. Stir back into the stew and repeat if need be. You could also remove the lid for the last 30 mins or so and turn the slow cooker up if you want to thicken a sauce a bit.

Notes & conversion tables

NOTES ON THE RECIPES
- Eggs are large in the UK and Australia and extra large in America unless stated.
- Wash fresh produce before preparation.
- Recipes contain nutritional analyses for 'sugars', which means the total sugar content including all natural sugars in the ingredients, unless otherwise stated.

APPROXIMATE LIQUID CONVERSION

Metric	Imperial	Aus	US
50ml	2 fl oz	¼ cup	¼ cup
125ml	4 fl oz	½ cup	½ cup
175ml	6 fl oz	¾ cup	¾ cup
225ml	8 fl oz	1 cup	1 cup
300ml	10 fl oz/½ pint	½ pint	1¼ cups
450ml	16 fl oz	2 cups	2 cups/1 pint
600ml	20 fl oz/1 pint	1 pint	2½ cups
1 litre	35 fl oz/1¾ pints	1¾ pints	1 quart

OVEN TEMPERATURE CONVERSION

GAS	°C	°C FAN	°F	OVEN TEMP.
¼	110	90	225	Very cool
½	120	100	250	Very cool
1	140	120	275	Cool or slow
2	150	130	300	Cool or slow
3	160	140	325	Warm
4	180	160	350	Moderate
5	190	170	375	Moderately hot
6	200	180	400	Fairly hot
7	220	200	425	Hot
8	230	210	450	Very hot
9	240	220	475	Very hot

APPROXIMATE WEIGHT CONVERSIONS
Cup measurements, which are used in Australia and America, have not been listed here as they vary from ingredient to ingredient. Kitchen scales should be used to measure dry/solid ingredients.

SPOON MEASURES
Spoon measurements are level unless otherwise specifed.
- 1 teaspoon (tsp) = 5ml
- 1 tablespoon (tbsp) = 15ml
- 1 Australian tablespoon = 20ml (cooks in Australia should measure 3 teaspoons where 1 tablespoon is specifed in a recipe)

Good Food is concerned about sustainable sourcing and animal welfare. Where possible, humanely reared meats, sustainably caught fish (see fishonline.org for further information from the Marine Conservation Society) and free- range chickens and eggs are used when recipes are originally tested.

What we mean by healthy

At *Good Food* we believe that a varied, balanced diet featuring whole foods is the key to good health. Everyone's needs are different, so we provide the information and recipes to help you create healthy habits.

At *Good Food* we make our healthy recipes as nutritious as they are delicious. Here we explain our approach to healthy eating, and how we label our recipes.

Our recipes are labelled **healthy** in the good to know section if they meet all of the following criteria per serving:
Saturated fat: No more than 5g
Sugar: No more than 15g
Salt: No more than 1.5g

Our healthy recipes are also checked to ensure they have low-to-medium levels of fat, saturated fat, sugar and salt per 100g. If the recipe was a packaged product, it would carry a green or amber colour coding.

Please note: Ingredients listed as serving suggestions are not included in the nutritional analysis.

Giving the info you need

We list the number of kcals, fat, saturates, carbs, sugars, fibre, protein and salt per serving. On some recipes we also highlight 'good to know' information when a recipe is healthy, vegetarian, vegan, low-fat, low-calorie, gluten-free, high in fibre or a source of omega-3. We note how many portions of fruit and veg are in a serving, and when the recipe contains more than a third of your daily recommended amount of key nutrients (calcium, folate, vitamin C and iron).

A NOTE ON FAT
Fat is an essential part of a balanced diet. However, it's advisable to cut down on saturated fats and trans fats, replacing these with healthier unsaturated varieties like rapeseed and olive oil, plus healthy food sources like nuts and seeds. Fat helps us to absorb key vitamins, and omega-3 fats – found in oily fish – are essential in small amounts because we can't produce them in our bodies.

WHAT ABOUT SUGAR?
We list total sugars, which includes sugars occurring naturally in foods (like lactose in milk), as well as those added to a recipe, such as refined table sugar and honey. It is these added sugars, known as 'free' sugars, that we are advised to cut back on.

DAILY GUIDELINES
Your doctor or health professional may have given you a calorie and nutrient goal. You could also compare the per-serving amounts on recipes with the Reference Intakes (RI) – the official amount an average adult should consume daily.

Energy: 2,000 kcals
Protein: 50g
Carbohydrates: 260g
Sugar: 90g
Fat: 70g
Saturates: 20g
Salt: 6g

Please note: RIs for total fat, saturates, sugar and salt are maximum daily amounts for adults.

LOW-CALORIE RECIPES
Starter, snack, drink or dessert = 150 kcals or less
Breakfasts = 250 kcals or less
Complete main meal with sides = 500 kcals or less

All health content is provided for general information only and should not be treated as a substitute for the medical advice of your own doctor or any other health care professional. If you have any concerns about your general health you should contact your local health care provider. See our website terms and conditions for more information.

Health benefits

Find out what some of the ingredients you eat do for you...

BLUEBERRIES

Blueberries are high in vitamin C, which helps protect cells and aids the absorption of iron, and contain soluble fibre, which is beneficial to the digestive system.

Blueberries are extremely rich in phytochemicals, naturally occurring plant compounds, such as ellagic acid and anthocyanins, which are responsible for the blue, indigo and red colouring. Phytochemicals have been extensively researched for their antioxidant content, which has been linked to numerous health benefits.

Blueberries are low in calories and a 100g serving provides 2.4g fibre. A wide range of colourful fruits and vegetables are encouraged as part of a balanced diet and blueberries are a good choice to include. One portion of blueberries is about a handful.

Eat them with the porridge recipes on p18–25 and the rice pudding on p26.

SPINACH

Spinach is well known for its nutritional qualities and has always been regarded as a plant with remarkable abilities to restore energy, increase vitality and improve the quality of the blood. There are sound reasons why spinach would produce such results, primarily the fact that it is rich in iron. Iron plays a central role in the function of red blood cells, which help in transporting oxygen around the body, in energy production and DNA synthesis. Spinach is also an excellent source of vitamin K, vitamin A, vitamin C and folate as well as being a good source of manganese, magnesium, iron and vitamin B2.

Stir spinach in at the end of the cooking time on the recipes that use it or add it to any of your favourite curries and stews.

ALMONDS

If you avoid dairy, calcium-rich almonds are a good choice to ensure you're getting enough of this bone-building mineral. Almonds are also high in vitamin E, a nutrient that can help to improve the condition and appearance of your skin. For extra heart health benefits, swap flaked almonds for the whole nut - with the skin intact - because the almond's skin is full of heart-protecting compounds called flavonoids.

Scatter almonds on porridges, Middle-Eastern-inspired dishes and curries.

PISTACHIOS

Being especially rich in vitamin B6, which is important for keeping hormones balanced and healthy, pistachios are thought to be a good option for those with problem periods. They also contain the antioxidants lutein and zeaxanthin, which play an important role in protecting the eyes.

Pistachios add a ping of green colour to tagines and stews and you can add them to rich meat such venison and lamb.

BEETROOT

Beetroot's deep purple colour comes from plant chemicals called betalains. Like anthocyanins, betalains have antioxidant and anti-inflammatory properties. You can also find betalains in the stems of chard and rhubarb but it's the flesh and skin of beetroots that are especially rich in them.

Beetroot is also a good source of vitamins and minerals, including folate, iron, manganese and potassium. They're also nitrate-rich, which contributes to many of beetroot's perceived health benefits. For example, a study from 2013 found that consuming beetroot juice was linked with lower blood pressure.

Try beetroot in the slow-cooked beetroot and beef curry on p178.

STRAWBERRIES

Strawberries are an excellent source of vitamins C and K as well as providing a good dose of fibre, folate, manganese and potassium. They have been used throughout history in a medicinal context to help with digestive ailments, teeth whitening and skin irritations. Their fibre and fructose content may help regulate blood sugar levels by slowing digestion and the fibre is thought to have a satiating effect. Leaves can be eaten raw, cooked or used to make tea.

The vibrant red colour of strawberries is due to large amounts of anthocyanins, which also means they contain powerful antioxidants and are thought to protect against inflammation, cancer and heart disease.

Add strawberries to your breakfast porridge or rice pudding or eat them with a bowl of freshly made yoghurt on p30.

GARLIC

The garlic bulb is the most commonly used portion of the plant, composed of 8-20 individual, teardrop-shaped cloves enclosed in a white parchment-like skin. It is an excellent source of vitamin B6 (pyridoxine). It is also a very good source of manganese, selenium and vitamin C. In addition, garlic is a good source of other minerals, including phosphorous, calcium, potassium, iron and copper. Many of the perceived therapeutic effects of garlic are thought to be due to its active ingredient allicin. This sulphur-containing compound gives garlic its distinctive pungent smell and taste. Luckily for us foodies, the action of chopping or crushing garlic supposedly stimulates the production of allicin, however it is thought that cooking garlic inhibits the formation of some of the perceived medicinal properties.

Garlic is included in many of the recipes in this book, if you want to include more in your diet then add some freshly chopped garlic as a garnish.

Chapter 1:

BREAKFASTS AND BRUNCH

A nourishing morning meal helps to get your day off to the best possible start. If you like a hot breakfast but don't have time to stand over the stove in the morning, a slow cooker can be your best friend. Our porridge recipes cook in just 20-30 minutes, so you can leave the ingredients to cook while you get ready. Try our classic creamy slow-cooked porridge or shake things up with our cardamom and peach quinoa porridge for a fresh start to the day. And it's not just for rushed mornings – a slow cooker brunch is a brilliant, fuss-free way to enjoy your lazy weekend mornings. Our brunch options include baked Turkish breakfast eggs or low-and-slow breakfast beans.

Slow-cooked porridge

Put this oaty breakfast into your slow cooker while you get ready in the morning. Add your favourite toppings. You can use any cup of about 250ml to make this, just make sure you use the same one for the oats and milk.

 TAKES 40 mins   SERVES 4

- 4 cups milk (or half milk, half water for a less creamy version), plus a dribble more milk to serve
- jumbo oats
- ¼ cup dried fruits (optional)

TO SERVE
- your favourite toppings – brown sugar or honey, sliced bananas, grated apple, blueberries, pinch cinnamon, natural yogurt, etc

1 Heat the slow cooker if necessary. Heat the milk to boiling point. Put the oats in the bowl of the slow cooker along with a pinch of salt, then pour over the milk, or a mixture of milk and boiling water. Add the dried fruit, if using. Cook on High for 20–30 mins.

2 Give the porridge a really good stir. Add a drop more milk if necessary, then ladle into bowls and add your favourite toppings.

GOOD TO KNOW vegetarian • gluten-free • low-fat • healthy
PER SERVING kcals 264 • fat 7g • saturates 3g • carbs 33g • sugars 11g • fibre 4g • protein 15g • salt 0.4g

Porridge with blueberry compote

Top high-fibre porridge oats with creamy Greek yogurt and healthy blueberries – buy frozen to help cut the cost of this filling breakfast

⏱ TAKES 40 mins 🍴 SERVES 2

- 6 tbsp porridge oats
- just under ½ x 200ml tub 0% fat Greek-style yogurt
- 175g blueberries, fresh or frozen
- 1 tsp honey

1 Heat the slow cooker if necessary. Heat the milk to boiling point. Put the oats in the bowl of the slow cooker along with a pinch of salt, then pour over the milk, or a mixture of milk and boiling water. Cook on High for 20–30 mins. Stir in one third of the yoghurt.

2 Meanwhile, tip the blueberries into a pan with 1 tbsp water and the honey if using and gently poach until the blueberries have thawed (if frozen) and they are tender, but still holding their shape.

3 Spoon the porridge into bowls, top with the remaining yogurt and spoon over the blueberries.

GOOD TO KNOW vegetarian • healthy • low-fat • low-calorie
PER SERVING kcals 168 • fat 2g • saturates 1g • carbs 24g • sugars 9g • fibre 5g • protein 9g • salt 0g

Apple and linseed porridge

Start the day the right way with a nutrient-packed oaty breakfast – full of stomach-friendly fibre, great for digestion. This will reheat the following day if you only need enough for two people, add a splash more milk and heat it gently on the stove top or in a microwave.

 TAKES 40 mins SERVES 4

- 500ml skimmed milk
- 100g porridge oats
- 2 eating apples, peeled and grated
- ½ tsp ground cinnamon, plus extra for sprinkling
- 2 tbsp ground linseed
- 150ml yogurt
- drizzle of honey or agave syrup

1 Heat the slow cooker if necessary. Bring the milk to a boil. Put the oats, apples, cinnamon and milk in the slow cooker. Cook on High for 20–30 mins.
2 Stir in the ground linseeds, then divide into 4 breakfast bowls. Top each with a dollop of yogurt, a drizzle of honey or agave syrup, and a sprinkle more cinnamon.

GOOD TO KNOW vegetarian • healthy
PER SERVING kcals 168 • fat 2g • saturates 1g • carbs 24g • sugars 9g • fibre 5g • protein 9g • salt 0g

Cardamom and peach quinoa porridge

A breakfast of oats and quinoa with fresh ripe peach. Almond milk makes its suitable for dairy-free and vegan diets

 TAKES 40 mins SERVES 4

- 500ml unsweetened almond milk
- 150g quinoa
- 50g porridge oats
- 4 cardamom pods
- 3 ripe peaches, cut into slices
- 2 tsp maple syrup

1 Heat the slow cooker if necessary. Heat the almond milk to a simmer. Put the quinoa, oats and cardamom pods in the bowl with 250ml boiling water and the almond milk. Cook on High for 20–30 mins.
2 Remove the cardamom pods, spoon into bowls or jars and top with the peaches and maple syrup.

GOOD TO KNOW vegetarian • vegan • low-calorie • low-fat
PER SERVING kcals 231 • fat 4g • saturates 1g • carbs 37g • sugars 10g • fibre 6g • protein 8g • salt 0.2g

Slow cooker rice pudding

Rice pudding makes a filling, nutritious and gluten-free alternative to porridge for breakfast, especially when made without sugar. Add naturally sweet-tasting spices like cinnamon or vanilla and top with fresh or frozen berries, grated pear or a delicious and warming fruit compote.

 TAKES 4¼ hours · SERVES 6

- 1 tsp butter
- 1 litre semi-skimmed milk
- 200g wholegrain rice
- nutmeg or cinnamon
- 1 tbsp honey, a handful toasted, flaked almonds and fruit, to serve

1 Butter the slow cooker all over the base and half way up the sides. Heat the milk to simmering point. Mix the pudding rice with the milk and pour it into the slow cooker. Add a grating of nutmeg or cinnamon. Cook for 3½–4 hours on High and stir once or twice if you can.
2 Serve with honey, flaked almonds and fruit if you like.

GOOD TO KNOW low-calorie (as a breakfast) • low-fat • healthy • vegetarian • gluten-free
NUTRITION (per serving) kcals 200 • fat 4g • saturates 2g • carbs 32g • sugars 8g • fibre 1g • protein 8g • salt 0.2g

Spiced apples with barley

Use eating apples for this recipe if you want the rings to stay intact, cooking apples like Bramleys will turn to purée very quickly. Add 160g seasonal berries to supply natural sweetness, add fibre and make this 1 of your 5 a day.

 TAKES 2¼ hours SERVES 4

- ½ cup barley
- 2 eating apples
- ½ tsp cinnamon
- a grating of fresh nutmeg
- finely grated zest 1 large orange
- 4 tablespoons natural yogurt

1 Heat the slow cooker if necessary. Put the barley and 750ml boiling water into the slow cooker. Peel and core the apples so you have a hole the size of a pound coin in each one. Cut each apple in half.
2 Stand the apples skin side down on the barley. Mix the cinnamon, nutmeg and orange zest, and sprinkle them over the apples.
3 Cook on Low for 2 hours. Serve with natural yogurt.

Easy bio yogurt

Live yogurt is full of probiotics, the good bacteria that can help to promote good gut health, and it can easily be made in a slow cooker. You just need two ingredients, milk and some live yogurt as a starter. If you are short of prep time you can skip the first couple of hours by heating the milk in a pan.

 TAKES 17½ hours   MAKES 2 litres

- 2 litres whole milk
- 100ml live yogurt, either shop bought or from a previous homemade batch

1 Tip the milk into the slow cooker. Cover and heat on High until the temperature of the milk reaches 82C, this will take a couple of hours. Turn off the slow cooker and allow the temperature to drop to 43C for a further 2–3 hours. Take a mugful of the warm milk and mix it with the yogurt then pour the mixture back into the slow cooker and stir really well. Cover, wrap the slow cooker in a big towel and then leave undisturbed for 9–12 hours until the mixture has set.

2 Eat on top of cereal or porridge, topped with fresh fruit, in marinades or drink in smoothies. If you want it thicker, for dips for example, line a large sieve with muslin and place it over a bowl, tip in the yogurt and allow some of the whey to strain off until you get the consistency of yogurt that you like. The longer you leave it the thicker it will become. Store in the fridge for up to 2 weeks.

GOOD TO KNOW vegetarian • gluten-free
PER SERVING kcals 120 • fat 5g • saturates 3g • carbs 11g • sugars 11g • fibre 0g • protein 8g • salt 0.3g

Baked Turkish breakfast eggs

In America this would be known as a breakfast casserole and baked either in the oven or, as here, in a slow cooker. Studies suggest that eggs make a great breakfast choice – they provide sustained energy so you won't be tempted mid-morning and they enhance brain function, concentration and even lift mood.

 TAKES 6¼ hours SERVES 4

- 1 tbsp olive oil
- 2 onions, finely sliced
- 1 red pepper, cored and finely sliced
- 1 small red chilli, finely sliced
- 8 cherry tomatoes
- 1 slice sourdough bread, cubed
- 4 eggs
- 2 tbsp skimmed milk
- small bunch parsley, finely chopped
- 4 tbsp natural yogurt, to serve

1 Oil the inside of a small slow cooker and heat if necessary. Heat the remaining oil in a heavy-based frying pan. Stir in the onions, pepper and chilli. Cook until they begin to soften. Tip into the slow cooker and add the cherry tomatoes and bread and stir everything. Season.
2 Whisk the eggs with the milk and parsley and pour this over the top, making sure all the other ingredients are covered. Cook for 5-6 hours. Serve with the yogurt.

GOOD TO KNOW 2 of 5 a day • low-calorie (as a breakfast) • vegetarian • healthy • high in vitamin C
PER SERVING kcals 165 • fat 8g • saturates 2g • carbs 13g • sugars 7g • fibre 3g • protein 9g • salt 0.32g

Low-and-slow breakfast beans

Enjoy over toast or as a side with eggs. Leave the garlic out if you prefer. Beans are a good source of vegetarian protein as well as slow-releasing carbs – making them a smart breakfast choice.

🕑 TAKES 5½ hours 🕑 SERVES 4

- 1 tbsp olive oil
- 1 onion, thinly sliced
- 2 garlic cloves, chopped
- 1 tbsp white or red wine vinegar
- 1 heaped tbsp soft brown sugar
- 400g can pinto beans, drained and rinsed
- 200ml passata
- small bunch coriander, chopped

1 Heat the slow cooker if necessary. Heat the oil in a large frying pan and fry the onion until it starts to brown, then add the garlic and cook for 1 min. Add the vinegar and sugar and bubble for a minute. Stir in the beans and passata and season with black pepper. Tip everything into the slow cooker.

2 Cook on Low for 5 hours. If the sauce seems a little thin turn the heat to High and cook for a few more minutes. Stir through the coriander.

GOOD TO KNOW 2 of 5 a day • gluten-free • low-fat • vegetarian
PER SERVING kcals 149 • fat 3g • saturates 0.5g • carbs 21g • sugars 12g • fibre 5g • protein 6g • salt 0.39g

Chicken congee

This savoury, Asian version of our much loved porridge makes a wonderful breakfast or comforting dinner. The exact consistency of congee is a personal preference, like porridge, you can cook it for longer with the lid off to thicken it.

🕐 TAKES 10½ hours 🕐 SERVES 2

- 1 cup long grain rice
- 100g cooked, shredded chicken
- a thumb-sized piece ginger, finely chopped
- 2 spring onions, thinly sliced
- 25g roasted peanuts, crushed, to serve
- few sprigs of coriander
- sriracha, to serve

FOR THE SOY EGGS (OPTIONAL)
- 2 eggs
- 300ml soy sauce
- 1 tbsp granulated sugar

1 If you are making the soy eggs, boil the eggs for 6 mins, then cool under cold running water. When cool enough to handle, peel the eggs. Mix the soy with the sugar, stirring well so that the sugar dissolves. Pour in 75ml water then add the eggs and leave in the soy mixture for at least 2 hours or overnight. You may need to put a small plate on top of the eggs to keep them submerged, as they'll be bobbing around.

2 Meanwhile, heat the slow cooker if necessary. Place the rice in a small bowl and wash in running cold water until the water turns clear and doesn't look milky. Put the rice in the cooker with 8 cups water, cover and cook on Low for 8–10 hours. You want it to be soupy, like a wet risotto.

3 When the rice is cooked, season to taste and stir in the shredded chicken and chopped ginger. Divide the congee between 2 bowls. Scatter over the chopped spring onions and crushed peanuts. Top with the soy egg halves if using, and a sprig of coriander. Drizzle the sriracha over and extra soy sauce if you like.

GOOD TO KNOW healthy
PER SERVING kcals 557 • fat 28g • saturates 11g • carbs 41g • sugars 3g • fibre 2g • protein 34g • salt 4g

Chapter 2:

SOUPS AND BROTHS

· ·

Who doesn't love a bowl of hot, comforting soup? We've put together a few of our favourite recipes for silky smooth blends, chunky soups and noodle-packed broths – all full of nourishing, flavourful ingredients. We've even included a chorizo-topped option that's so delicious, no one will guess that it's healthy.

Spiced carrot and lentil soup

A delicious, spicy blend, packed full of iron and low fat to boot. This recipe is easily doubled.

🕐 TAKES 3½ hours 🕐 SERVES 4

- 2 tsp cumin seeds
- pinch dried chilli flakes
- 2 tbsp olive oil
- 600g/1lb 5 carrots, washed and coarsely grated (no need to peel)
- 140g/5 red split lentils
- 700ml/1¼ hot vegetable stock
- 125ml/4 milk
- plain yogurt and warmed naan breads, to serve

1 Heat the slow cooker if necessary. Put half the cumin seeds, half the chilli flakes, the oil, carrots, lentils and stock in the pot. Cover and cook on High for 3 hours until the lentils are tender.
2 Dry-fry the remaining cumin seeds and chilli flakes just until fragrant.
3 When the lentils are done, stir in the milk and whizz the soup with a stick blender or in a food processor until smooth (or leave it chunky, if you prefer). Add a splash of water if the soup is a bit thick for you. Season to taste and finish with a dollop of yogurt and a sprinkling of the toasted spices. Serve with warmed naan breads.

GOOD TO KNOW healthy • vegetarian
PER SERVING kcals 238g • fat 7g • saturates 1g • carbs 34g • sugars 0g • fibre 5g • protein 11g • salt 0.25g

Courgette, potato and cheddar soup

This freezable soup is a delicious way to use up a glut of courgettes.

⏱ TAKES 4 hours 🕐 SERVES 8

- 500g potatoes, unpeeled and roughly chopped
- 2 vegetable stock cubes
- 1kg courgettes, roughly chopped
- bunch spring onions, sliced – save 1 for serving, if eating straight away
- 100g extra-mature cheddar or vegetarian alternative, grated, plus a little extra to serve
- good grating fresh nutmeg

1 Heat the slow cooker if necessary. Put the potatoes in the slow cooker pot with just enough water to cover them and crumble in the stock cubes. Cover and cook for 3 hours on High until the potatoes are tender.

2 Scoop out a couple of ladlefuls of stock and save for the end. Add the courgettes and spring onions, put the lid back on and cook for 30 mins more until the courgettes are tender.

3 Take off the heat, then stir in the cheese and season with the nutmeg, salt and some black pepper. Whizz to a thick soup with a stick blender, adding the reserved stock until you get the consistency you like. Serve scattered with the extra grated cheddar, spring onions and black pepper. Or cool and freeze in freezer bags or containers with good lids for up to 3 months.

GOOD TO KNOW healthy • vegetarian
PER SERVING kcals 131 • fat 6g • saturates 3g • carbs 14g • sugars 3g • fibre 2g • protein 7g • salt 1.31g

Curried lentil, parsnip and apple soup

This spicy soup combines red lentils, apples and parsnip for a smooth, warming soup – a low fat meal that you can make ahead and freeze. If you have a small slow cooker then halve the recipe.

 TAKES 3½ hours SERVES 6–8

- 2 tbsp sunflower oil
- 3 tbsp medium curry paste
- 2 medium onions, roughly chopped
- 500g parsnips (around 5 medium parsnips), peeled and cut into chunks
- 140g dried red lentils
- 2 Bramley apples
- (about 400g), peeled, cored and cut into chunks
- 1 litre vegetable or chicken stock, made with 1 stock cube
- natural yogurt and coriander leaves, to serve (optional)

1 Heat the slow cooker if necessary. Heat the oil in a large saucepan and fry the curry paste and onions together over a medium heat for 3 mins, stirring. Add the parsnips, lentils and apple. Pour over the stock and bring to a simmer.
2 Tip into the slow cooker, cover and cook on Low for 3 hours until the vegetables are tender.
3 Blitz with a stick blender until smooth. (Or leave to cool for a few mins, then blend in a food processor.) Adjust the seasoning to taste, and if it is a little thick dilute with boiling water to your desired consistency. Serve with yogurt and garnish with fresh coriander, if you like.

GOOD TO KNOW healthy • vegetarian
PER SERVING kcals 204 • fat 5g • saturates 1g • carbs 24g • sugars 10g • fibre 8g • protein 12g
• salt 0.7g

Creamy tomato soup

A low-fat, vegetarian soup that everyone will love – passata and whole milk give a silky smooth finish.

⏱ TAKES 3½ hours ◔ SERVES 6 Can be frozen

- 1½ tbsp olive oil
- 1 onion, chopped
- 1 celery stick, chopped
- 140g carrots, chopped
- 250g potato, diced
- 2 bay leaves
- 2½ tbsp tomato purée
- 1 tbsp golden caster sugar
- 1 tbsp red or white wine vinegar
- 2 x 400g cans chopped tomatoes
- 250ml passata
- 1 vegetable stock cube
- 200ml full-fat milk

1 Heat the slow cooker if necessary. Put the oil and onion in a frying pan, and cook gently for 10–15 mins until the onion is softened. Boil the kettle.
2 Scrape the onion into the slow cooker pot with the celery, carrots, potatoes, bay leaves, tomato purée, sugar, vinegar, chopped tomatoes and passata. Crumble in the stock cube. Add 300ml boiling water. Cover and cook on High for 3 hours until the potato is tender, then remove the bay leaves.
3 Purée the soup with a stick blender (or ladle into a food processor in batches) until very smooth. Season to taste and add a pinch more sugar if it needs it. The soup can now be cooled and chilled for up to 2 days, or frozen for up to 3 months.
4 To serve, reheat the soup, stirring in the milk until hot – try not to let it boil.

GOOD TO KNOW healthy • vegetarian
PER SERVING kcals 180 • fat 6g • saturates 2g • carbs 26g • sugars 17g • fibre 5g • protein 6g • salt 1.2g

Thai chicken soup

Create a mouth-watering chicken soup with leftovers from your roast lunch.

🕐 TAKES 8 hours 🕔 SERVES 4

- 140g soba or wholewheat noodles
- 100g beansprouts
- 2 pak choi, leaves separated
- 1 red chilli, deseeded and sliced
- ½ tbsp low-salt soy sauce
- 2 tbsp honey
- juice 1 lime, plus wedges to serve
- 4 spring onions, sliced to garnish
- ½ small bunch mint leaves, shredded to garnish

FOR THE BROTH
- 1 roasted chicken carcass
- thumb-sized piece ginger, bashed and sliced
- 1 garlic clove, crushed
- 2 spring onions, sliced
- 5 peppercorns

1 To make the broth, heat the slow cooker if necessary. Put the chicken carcass in the slow cooker pot. Just cover it with hot water, then add the rest of the broth ingredients, and cover and cook on Low for 6–7 hours.
2 Strain the chicken broth into a clean pan. Carefully pick out any pieces of chicken and return them to the broth, but discard the bones. Put the broth back in the slow cooker pot.
3 Add the noodles, beansprouts, pak choi, red chilli, soy sauce, honey and lime juice, adding the squeezed lime halves to the pot, too. Cook on High, covered, for 30 mins more.
4 Ladle the soup into bowls, scatter over the spring onions and mint leaves, and serve with the lime wedges for squeezing over.

GOOD TO KNOW 1 of 5 a day · low-fat, healthy · good source of folate
PER SERVING kcals 207 · fat 2g · saturates 0.1g · carbs 37g · sugars 12g · fibre 5g · protein 8g · salt 1.22g

Hot and sour broth with prawns

This healthy starter is a palate cleansing way to kick off a Chinese meal. The recipe is nice and simple and looks gorgeous. Add 300g more vegetables such as blanched bean sprouts, shredded carrot, peas or spinach to make this even healthier and reach 1 of your 5-a-day.

🕐 TAKES 1½ hours 🕐 SERVES 4

- 3 tbsp rice vinegar or white wine vinegar
- 500ml low-salt chicken stock
- ½ tbsp low-salt soy sauce
- 1–2 tbsp golden caster sugar
- thumb-sized piece ginger, peeled and thinly sliced
- 2 small hot red chillies, thinly sliced
- 3 spring onions, thinly sliced
- 300g small raw peeled prawns, from a sustainable source

1 Heat the slow cooker if necessary. Put the vinegar, stock, soy sauce, sugar (start with 1 tablespoon and add the second at the end if you want the soup sweeter), ginger and chillies in the slow cooker pot. Cover and cook on High for 1 hour, or on Low for 4–8 hours, if you have time.

2 When you're nearly ready to serve, add the spring onions and prawns. Cover and cook on High for 20–30 mins until the prawns are just cooked.

GOOD TO KNOW low-calorie • low-fat • healthy
PER SERVING kcals 93 • fat 1g • saturates 0.4g • carbs 7g • sugars 6g • fibre 0.2g • protein 14g • salt 0.69g

Moroccan chickpea soup

A Moroccan chickpea soup packed with veg, this makes a good vegetarian starter.

TAKES 5 hours SERVES 4

- 1 tbsp olive oil
- 1 small onion, chopped
- 2 celery sticks, chopped
- 2 tsp ground cumin
- 300ml hot vegetable stock
- 400g can chopped tomatoes with garlic
- 400g can chickpeas, rinsed and drained
- 100g frozen broad beans, defrosted
- zest and juice ½ lemon
- large handful coriander or parsley and flatbread, to serve

1 Heat the slow cooker if necessary. Heat the oil in a large saucepan, then fry the onion and celery gently for 10 mins until softened, stirring frequently. Tip in the cumin and fry for another min.

2 Tip into the slow cooker, then add the stock and tomatoes, plus a good grind of black pepper. Cook on Low for 4 hours. Throw in the chickpeas and broad beans and lemon juice, cook for a further 30 mins. Season, then top with a sprinkling of lemon zest and chopped herbs. Serve with flatbread.

GOOD TO KNOW healthy • vegetarian
PER SERVING kcals 148 • fat 5g • saturates 1g • carbs 17g • sugars 0g • fibre 6g • protein 9g • salt 1.07g

Chunky minestrone soup

The perfect solution to a cold night in? A warming bowl of this home-made chunky soup.

🕐 TAKES 7 hours   🕐 SERVES 4

- 3 large carrots
- 1 large onion
- 4 celery sticks
- 1 tbsp olive oil
- 2 garlic cloves, crushed
- 2 large potatoes, cut into small dice
- 2 tbsp tomato purée
- 1 litre vegetable stock
- 400g can chopped tomatoes
- 400g can butter or cannellini beans, drained
- 140g spaghetti, snapped into short lengths
- ½ head Savoy cabbage, shredded
- crusty bread, to serve

1 Heat the slow cooker if necessary. Rougly chop and then whizz the carrots, onion and celery into small pieces in a food processor or finely chop them by hand. Heat the oil in a pan, add the processed vegetables, garlic and potatoes, then cook over a high heat for 5 mins until softened. Tip into the slow cooker.

2 Stir in the tomato purée, stock and tomatoes. Cook on Low for 6 hours.

3 Tip in the beans and pasta, then cook for a further 30 minutes on High, adding the cabbage for the final 5 mins. Season to taste and serve with crusty bread.

GOOD TO KNOW high in fibre • good source of iron and folate • vegetarian • healthy
PER SERVING kcals 420 • fat 6g • saturates 1g • carbs 79g • sugars 24g • fibre 16g • protein 18g
• salt 1.11g

Hearty mushroom soup

A satisfying and low-fat vegetarian soup that's a good source of folate.

⏱ TAKES 6½ hours ◔ SERVES 4-6

- 25g pack porcini mushrooms
- 2 tbsp olive oil
- 1 medium onion, finely diced
- 2 large carrots, diced
- 2 garlic cloves, finely chopped
- 1 tbsp chopped rosemary, or 1 tsp dried
- 500g fresh mushrooms, such as chestnut, finely chopped
- 600ml vegetable stock (from a cube is fine)
- 2 tbsp Marsala or dry sherry
- 2 tbsp tomato purée
- 100g pearl barley
- grated fresh Parmesan, to serve (optional)

1 Heat the slow cooker if necessary. Put the porcini in a bowl with 250ml boiling water and leave to soak for 25 mins. Meanwhile heat the oil in a pan and add the onion, carrot, garlic, rosemary and seasoning. Fry for 5 mins on a medium heat until softened and tip into the slow cooker. Drain the porcini, saving the liquid, and finely chop. Tip into the frying pan with the fresh mushrooms, fry for another 5 mins, then add the stock, Marsala or sherry, tomato purée and strained porcini liquid and bring to a boil. Tip into the slow cooker.

2 Cook on Low for 5 hours and then add the barley and cook for a further 1 hour or until barley is soft. Serve in bowls with Parmesan sprinkled over, if you like.

GOOD TO KNOW healthy • vegetarian
PER SERVING kcals 245 • fat 7g • saturates 1g • carbs 35g • sugars 10g • fibre 3g • protein 8g • salt 1.13g

Pea and mint soup

A superhealthy starter or snack that's great hot or cold.

TAKES 5 hours SERVES 4

- 1 bunch spring onions, trimmed and roughly chopped
- 1 medium potato, peeled and diced
- 1 garlic clove, crushed
- 425ml low-salt vegetable or chicken stock
- 250g frozen peas
- 4 tbsp chopped fresh mint
- large pinch golden caster sugar
- 1 tbsp fresh lemon or lime juice
- 150ml buttermilk or soured cream

1 Heat the slow cooker if necessary. Put the spring onions, potato, garlic and stock into the slow cooker. Cook on Low for 4 hours. For the garnish, blanch 3 tbsp of the peas in boiling water for 2–3 mins, drain, put in a bowl of cold water and set aside. Add the remaining peas to the soup base and cook for 30 mins.

2 Stir in the mint, sugar and lemon or lime juice, cool slightly then pour into a food processor or liquidiser and whizz until as smooth as you like. Stir in half the buttermilk or soured cream, taste and season with salt and pepper.

3 To serve the soup cold, cool quickly, then chill – you may need to add more stock to the soup before serving as it will thicken as it cools. To serve hot, reheat without boiling (to prevent the buttermilk or soured cream from curdling).

4 Serve the soup in bowls, garnished with the remaining buttermilk and the drained peas.

GOOD TO KNOW healthy • vegetarian
PER SERVING kcals 108 • fat 1g • saturates 1g • carbs 17g • sugars 1.6g • fibre 4g • protein 8g
• salt 0.84g

Red lentil and chorizo soup

Sweet smoked paprika and cumin flavour this rustic blend topped with spicy Spanish sausage.

⏱ TAKES 4½ hours 🥧 SERVES 6

- 1 tbsp olive oil, plus extra for drizzling
- 200g cooking chorizo, peeled and diced
- 1 large onion, chopped
- 2 carrots, chopped
- pinch cumin seeds
- 3 garlic cloves, chopped
- 1 tsp smoked paprika, plus extra for sprinkling
- pinch golden caster sugar
- small splash red wine vinegar
- 250g red lentils
- 2 x 400g cans chopped tomatoes
- 200ml low-salt chicken stock
- plain yogurt, to serve

1 Heat the slow cooker if necessary. Heat the oil in a large pan. Add the chorizo and cook until crisp and it has released its oils. Remove with a slotted spoon into a bowl, leaving the fat in the pan. Fry the onion, carrots and cumin seeds briefly until they just begin to colour, then add the garlic and fry for 1 min more. Scatter over the paprika and sugar, cook for 1 min, then splash in the vinegar. Tip everything into the slow cooker, then stir in the lentils and pour over the tomatoes and chicken stock. Cook on Low for 4 hours.

2 Blitz with a hand blender until smooth-ish but still chunky, add a little water if you need to thin it down. Can be made several days ahead or frozen for 6 months at this point. Serve in bowls, drizzled with yogurt and olive oil, scattered with the chorizo and a sprinkling of paprika.

GOOD TO KNOW Healthy
PER SERVING kcals 260 • Fat 13g • Saturates 5g • Carbs 16g • Sugars 10g • Fibre 7g • Protein 18g • Salt 1.1g

Spiced root soup with crisp spiced onions

Spiced root soup with crisp spiced onions – a hearty winter soup.

TAKES 4½ hours   SERVES 4 Can be froxen

- 2 onions
- 3 tbsp vegetable oil
- 1 tsp mustard seeds
- 1 tsp cumin seeds
- 2 leeks, sliced
- 3 carrots, sliced
- 2 medium potatoes, chopped
- 2 parsnips or 1 small celeriac, chopped
- 2–3 tsp curry paste
- 600ml vegetable stock (from granules or a cube)
- 250ml natural yogurt, plus extra to serve
- roughly chopped coriander or parsley, to serve

1 Heat the slow cooker if necessary. Peel and halve the onions through the root, then slice thinly lengthways. Heat 2 tbsp of the oil in a large pan, add half the onions and fry until just starting to colour. Add the mustard and cumin seeds and fry until nicely browned.

2 Add vegetables and curry paste and stir until well coated. Pour in the stock and bring to the boil. Tip into the slow cooker and cook on Low for 4 hours until the vegetables are tender. Meanwhile, heat the remaining tbsp of oil in a small pan, add the remaining onions and fry quickly until crisp and browned. Tip onto kitchen paper.

3 Purée the soup in batches, then return to the pan and stir in most of the yogurt. Taste and add salt, if necessary. Reheat gently, then ladle into bowls and top each with a spoonful of yogurt, some fried onions and a scattering of roughly chopped coriander or parsley.

GOOD TO KNOW healthy • vegetarian
PER SERVING kcals 240 • fat 13g • saturates 1g • carbs 25g • sugars 16g • fibre 7g • protein 9g • salt 1.45g

Red lentil carrot soup

This warming and budget-friendly vegetarian soup is perfect packed in a flask for lunch. It's also easy to double the quantities and freeze half for later.

 TAKES 4½ hours ◔ SERVES 2

- 1 white onion, finely sliced
- 2 tsp olive oil
- 3 garlic cloves, sliced
- 2 carrots, scrubbed and diced
- 85g red lentils
- 1 low-salt vegetable stock cube, crumbled
- generous sprigs parsley, chopped (about 2 tbsp), plus a few extra leaves

1 Heat the slow cooker if necessary. Put the kettle on to boil while you finely slice the onion. Heat the oil in a medium pan, add the onion and fry for 2 mins while you slice the garlic and dice the carrots. Add them to the pan, and cook briefly over the heat. Tip into the slow cooker.

2 Pour in 500ml of the boiling water from the kettle, stir in the lentils and stock cube, then cover the pot and cook on Low for 4 hours until the lentils are tender, adding a little more water if you need to. Turn off the heat and stir in the parsley. Ladle into bowls, and scatter with extra parsley leaves, if you like.

GOOD TO KNOW healthy • vegetarian
PER SERVING kcals 258 • fat 5g • saturates 1g • carbs 37g • sugars 12g • fibre 8g • protein 13g • salt 1.6g

Moroccan roasted vegetable soup

Roasted roots are perfect for making soup – we used parsnips, butternut squash and carrots, flavoured with ras el hanout spice mix.

⏱ TAKES 7 hours ⏳ SERVES 4–5

- 1 red onion, cut into 8 wedges
- 300g carrots, cut into 2cm chunks
- 300g parsnips, cut into 2cm chunks
- 300g peeled butternut squash, cut into 2cm chunks
- 1 small potato, cut into 2cm chunks
- 2 garlic cloves
- 1 tbsp ras el hanout
- 1½ tbsp olive oil
- 650ml hot vegetable stock
- 6 tbsp Greek-style yogurt and 1 tbsp finely chopped mint, to serve (optional)

1 Heat oven to 200C/180C fan/gas 6. Tip all the vegetables and the garlic into a roasting tin. Sprinkle over the ras el hanout and some seasoning, drizzle over the oil and give everything a good stir. Roast for 30–35 mins, turning the vegetables over halfway, until they're tender and starting to caramelise a little.

2 Meanwhile heat the slow cooker if necessary. Transfer the roasted veg to the slow cooker, pour over the hot stock and cook on Low for 6 hours. Purée the soup in a food processor, or in the pot with a hand blender, until smooth. Serve with a dollop of yogurt, a scattering of mint and a grinding of black pepper.

GOOD TO KNOW healthy · vegetarian
PER SERVING kcals 187 · fat 6g · saturates 1g · carbs 29g · sugars 17g · fibre 10g · protein 5g · salt 0.9g

Indian winter soup

This warming winter soup is high in fibre, low in fat and can be frozen for ultimate convenience.

🕐 TAKES 5½ hours 🕐 SERVES 4-6

- 100g pearl barley
- 2 tbsp vegetable oil
- ½ tsp brown mustard seeds
- 1 tsp cumin seeds
- 2 green chillies, deseeded and finely chopped
- 1 bay leaf
- 2 cloves
- 1 small cinnamon stick
- ½ tsp turmeric
- 1 large onion, chopped
- 2 garlic cloves, finely chopped
- 1 parsnip, cut into chunks
- 200g butternut squash, cut into chunks
- 200g sweet potato, cut into chunks
- 1 tsp paprika
- 1 tsp ground coriander
- 2 tomatoes, chopped
- 225g red lentils
- small bunch coriander, chopped
- 1 tsp grated ginger
- 1 tsp lemon juice

1 Heat the slow cooker if necessary. Rinse the pearl barley. Meanwhile, heat the oil in a frying pan. Fry the mustard seeds, cumin seeds, chillies, bay leaf, cloves, cinnamon and turmeric until fragrant and the seeds start to crackle. Tip in the onion and garlic, then cook for 1–2 mins. Tip everything into the slow cooker. Stir in the parsnip, butternut and sweet potato and mix thoroughly, making sure the vegetables are fully coated with the oil and spices. Sprinkle in the paprika, ground coriander and seasoning, and stir again.

2 Add the tomatoes and 800ml water. Cook on Low for 4 hours. Add the lentils and pearl barley and cook for a further 1 hour on Low. Stir in the chopped coriander, ginger and lemon juice.

GOOD TO KNOW healthy • vegan
PER SERVING kcals 445 • fat 8g • saturates 1g • carbs 80g • sugars 13g • fibre 8g • protein 19g
• salt 0.14g

Spiced black bean chicken soup with kale

Use up leftover roast or ready-cooked chicken in this healthy and warming South American-style soup, spiced up with cumin and chilli.

 TAKES 6 hours SERVES 4

- 2 tbsp mild olive oil
- 2 fat garlic cloves, crushed
- small bunch coriander stalks, finely chopped, leaves picked
- zest 1 lime, then cut into wedges
- 2 tsp ground cumin
- 1 tsp chilli flakes
- 400g can chopped tomatoes
- 300ml chicken stock
- 400g can black beans, rinsed and drained
- 175g kale, thick stalks removed, leaves shredded
- 250g leftover roast or ready-cooked chicken
- 50g feta, crumbled, to serve
- flour and corn tortillas, toasted, to serve

1 Heat the slow cooker if necessary. Heat the oil in a frying pan, add the garlic, coriander stalks and lime zest, then fry for 2 mins until fragrant. Stir in the cumin and chilli flakes, fry for 1 min more, tip everything into the slow cooker. Add the tomatoes and stock. Cook on Low for 4 hours. Add the beans and cook for another 1 hour on Low, then crush the beans against the bottom of the pot a few times using a potato masher. This will thicken the soup a little.

2 Stir the kale into the soup, cook for 30 mins or until tender, then tear in the chicken and let it heat through. Season to taste with salt, pepper and juice from half the lime, then serve in shallow bowls, scattered with the feta and a few coriander leaves. Serve the remaining lime in wedges for the table, with the toasted tortillas on the side.

GOOD TO KNOW healthy
PER SERVING kcals 293 • fat 11g • saturates 2g • carbs 15g • sugars 3g • fibre 6g • protein 26g • salt 1g

Butternut squash and sage soup

This vibrant orange pumpkin blend is a healthy way to warm up – served with herbs and a drizzle of honey.

🕐 TAKES 3½ hours 🥧 SERVES 8

- 1 tbsp olive oil
- 1 tbsp butter
- 3 onions, chopped
- 2 tbsp chopped sage
- 1.4kg peeled, deseeded butternut squash – buy whole squash and prepare, or buy bags of ready-prepared
- 1 tbsp clear honey
- 750ml vegetable stock
- bunch chives, snipped, and cracked black pepper to serve

1 Heat the slow cooker if necessary. Melt the oil and butter in a large saucepan or flameproof casserole. Add the onions and sage, and cook for a couple of minutes, then scrape into the slow cooker. Tip in the squash, honey and stock and cook on Low for 3 hours or until the squash is tender.

2 Let the soup cool a bit so you don't burn yourself, then whizz until really smooth with a hand blender, or in batches in a blender. Season, adding a drop more stock or water if the soup is too thick. Reheat before serving, sprinkled with chives and cracked black pepper.

GOOD TO KNOW healthy • vegetarian
PER SERVING kcals 130 • fat 4g • saturates 1g • carbs 21g • sugars 14g • fibre 5g • protein 3g • salt 0.5g

The ultimate makeover French onion soup

This French classic has had a makeover, losing the butter and beef stock to make a lighter soup that's still full of flavour.

 TAKES 15¾ hours ⊙ SERVES 4

FOR THE SOUP
- 4 large Spanish onions
- (about 900g)
- 3 tbsp extra virgin rapeseed oil
  4 thyme sprigs
- 2 bay leaves
- 150ml dry white wine
- 1 rounded tbsp plain flour
- 1 tbsp Swiss vegetable bouillon

FOR THE TOPPING
- 1 garlic clove, crushed
- 1 tbsp extra virgin rapeseed oil
- 4 long slices from a baguette
- 25g Parmesan, or vegetarian alternative, coarsely grated
- 50g Gruyère, coarsely grated

1 Heat the slow cooker if necessary. Cut the onions in half lengthways, then slice down into very thin slices. Put the oil and onions, 3 of the thyme sprigs and the bay leaves in the slow cooker. It will seem like a lot of onions, but they reduce right down. Cook on Low for 7 hours until the onions have reduced right down and are very soft.

2 When the onions are cooked, bring the wine to a boil in a small pan, then bubble away for 30 secs. Tip the flour into the onions and stir it in.

3 Gradually pour in the wine. Pour in 800ml boiling water. Stir in the bouillon, cook on Low for a further 8½ hours.

4 When the soup is ready, make the topping. Heat oven to 200C/180C fan/gas 6. Mix the garlic and the oil together. Brush all over the bread slices, then cut each one into cubes. Scatter over a baking sheet, then bake for 8–10 mins until golden. Set aside. Line a baking sheet with baking parchment or a sheet of non-stick silicone. Remove the leaves from the remaining thyme sprig, then mix with the grated Parmesan. Scatter and spread over the lined baking sheet into a 13 x 8cm rectangle. Bake for about 8 mins until melted and turning golden. Remove, leave to firm up, then snap into jagged pieces.

5 To serve, remove and discard the herbs from the soup. Ladle the soup into bowls – scatter over a few croutons, the Gruyère and a grinding of pepper, then perch a Parmesan crisp on top. Serve any remaining croutons separately.

GOOD TO KNOW healthy • vegetarian
PER SERVING kcals 405 • fat 19g • saturates 5g • carbs 44g • sugars 18g • fibre 4g • protein 12g • salt 1g

Carrot and ginger soup

Low-fat and warming, this bean and vegetable soup makes a healthy lunch or dinner. For a smarter look top with sliced almonds.

 TAKES 3½ hours · SERVES 4

- 1 tbsp rapeseed oil
- 1 large onion, chopped
- 2 tbsp coarsely grated ginger
- 2 garlic cloves, sliced
- ½ tsp turmeric nutmeg
- 425ml vegetable stock
- 500g carrots, sliced
- 400g can cannellini beans, drained

SUPERCHARGED TOPPING
- 4 tbsp almonds in their skins, cut into slivers
- sprinkle of nutmeg

1 Heat the slow cooker if necessary. Heat the oil in a frying pan, add the onion, ginger and garlic, and fry for 5 mins until starting to soften. Stir in the nutmeg and cook for 1 min more and tip into the slow cooker.

2 Pour in the stock, add the carrots and beans then cover and cook on Low for 3 hours until the carrots are tender.

3 Scoop a third of the mixture into a bowl and blitz the remainder with a hand blender or in a food processor until smooth. Return everything to the pan to re-heat. Serve topped with the almonds and nutmeg.

GOOD TO KNOW healthy · vegetarian
PER SERVING kcals 293 · fat 12g · saturates 1g · carbs 31g · sugars 19g · fibre 8g · protein 10g · salt 0.9g

Rustic vegetable soup

• •

This vegetarian soup is packed with vegetables and lentils – it's healthy, low fat and full of flavour. To bulk it up, why not add borlotti beans or chicken?

🕐 TAKES 5 hours 🍴 SERVES 4 Can be frozen

- 1 tbsp rapeseed oil
- 1 large onion, chopped
- 2 carrots, chopped
- 2 celery sticks, chopped
- 50g dried red lentils
- 750ml boiling vegetable bouillon
- 2 tbsp tomato purée
- 1 tbsp chopped fresh thyme
- 1 leek, finely sliced
- 175g bite-sized cauliflower florets
- 1 courgette, chopped
- 3 garlic cloves, finely chopped
- ½ large Savoy cabbage, stalks removed and leaves chopped
- 1 tbsp basil, chopped

1 Heat the slow cooker if necessary, Heat the oil in a large frying pan, add the onion, carrots and celery and fry for a few mins, stirring from time to time until they are starting to colour a little around the edges. Tip into the slow cooker. Stir in the lentils.

2 Pour in the hot bouillon, add the tomato purée and thyme and stir well. Add the leek, cauliflower, courgette and garlic, cover and cook on Low for 4 hours.

3 Add the cabbage and basil and cook for 30 mins more until the veg is just tender. Season with pepper, ladle into bowls and serve. Will keep in the fridge for a couple of days. Freezes well. Thaw, then reheat in a pan until piping hot.

• •

GOOD TO KNOW healthy • vegetarian
PER SERVING kcals 162 • fat 5g • saturates 1g • carbs 19g • sugars 9g • fibre 7g • protein 7g • salt 0.4g

Butternut soup with crispy sage and apple croutons

The apple and sage contrast beautifully with naturally sweet butternut squash in this low-fat, gluten-free festive dinner party starter

 TAKES 4½ hours SERVES 4

- 1 tbsp olive oil
- 1 large onion, chopped
- 1 garlic clove, chopped
- 1 tbsp Madeira or dry sherry
- 1 butternut squash, about 1kg, peeled, deseeded and chopped
- 250ml gluten-free vegetable stock, brought to a boil, plus a little extra if necessary
- 1 tsp chopped sage, plus 20 small leaves, cleaned and dried
- sunflower oil, for frying

FOR THE APPLE CROUTONS
- 1 tbsp olive oil
- 1 large eating apple, peeled, cored and diced
- few pinches golden caster sugar

1 Heat the slow cooker if necessary. Heat the oil in a frying pan, add the onion and fry for a couple of minutes. Add the garlic, cook for a minute, add the Madeira and bring it to a bubble and scrape everything into the slow cooker. Add the squash. Pour in the stock, stir in the chopped sage, then cover and cook on Low for 4 hours until the squash is tender.
2 Blitz with a hand blender or in a food processor until completely smooth. Will keep for 2 days or freeze for 3 months.
3 To make the crispy sage, heat some oil (a depth of about 2cm) in a small pan, then drop in the sage leaves and fry until they are crisp – you will need to do this in batches. Drain on kitchen paper. Will keep for several hours.
4 For the apple croutons, heat the oil in a large pan, add the apple and fry until starting to soften. Sprinkle with the sugar and stir until lightly caramelised.
5 To serve, ladle the soup into small bowls and top with the apple, sage and a grinding of black pepper.

GOOD TO KNOW healthy • gluten-free • vegan
PER SERVING kcals 231 • fat 7g • saturates 1g • carbs 31g • sugars 20g • fibre 8g • protein 4g • salt 0.4g

Herby chicken and butter bean soup

This rustic, chunky soup uses up leftover roast chicken and is packed with flavour from fresh rosemary, sage and thyme.

 TAKES 5 hours SERVES 6

- 1 tbsp olive or rapeseed oil
- 1 onion, chopped
- 4 carrots, chopped
- 3 sprigs rosemary, leaves picked and chopped
- 3 sprigs sage, leaves picked and chopped
- 3 sprigs thyme, leaves picked and chopped
- 2 tsp ground cumin
- 2 tsp ground coriander
- 1 tsp turmeric
- 1 tbsp plain flour
- 4 skinless chicken thighs
- 750ml chicken stock, brought to a boil
- 400g can butter bean, drained
- crusty bread, to serve

1 Heat the slow cooker if necessary. Heat the oil in a frying pan and add the onions, carrots, herbs, spices and flour, and stir for 1–2 mins to toast the spices. Tip everything into a slow cooker. Add the chicken thighs and stock. Stir well, cover and cook on Low for 4 hours.

2 Remove the chicken thighs from the cooker, shred the meat and discard the bones. Add the meat back into the soup, along with the butter beans, season and cook for a further 30 mins.

3 Use a hand-held blender to blitz the soup until smooth, leave it chunky or blend about half, so it's creamy but still has chunks of chicken, carrot and butter bean. Serve with extra pepper, and good crusty bread.

GOOD TO KNOW healthy
PER SERVING kcals 363 • fat 19g • saturates 4g • carbs 19g • sugars 11g • fibre 7g • protein 32g • salt 0.8g

Bean and barley soup

Low-fat, vegetarian and super-healthy, this filling one-pot lunch or dinner is packed with chickpeas, butter beans and pearl barley.

 TAKES 3 hours SERVES 4

- 2 tbsp vegetable oil
- 1 large onion, finely chopped
- 1 fennel bulb, quartered, cored and sliced
- 5 garlic cloves, crushed
- 400g can chickpeas, drained and rinsed
- 2 x 400g cans chopped tomatoes
- 300ml vegetable stock
- 250g pearl barley
- 215g can butter beans, drained and rinsed
- 100g baby spinach leaves grated Parmesan to serve

1 Heat the slow cooker if necessary. Heat the oil in a frying pan over a medium heat, add the onion, fennel and garlic, and cook until softened and just beginning to brown. Scrape them into the slow cooker.

2 Mash half the chickpeas and add to the pot with the tomatoes, stock and barley. Cook on Low for 2 hours or until the barley is tender.

3 Add the remaining chickpeas and the butter beans to the soup with the spinach and cook for another 30 mins. Season and serve scattered with Parmesan.

GOOD TO KNOW healthy • vegetarian • low-fat
PER SERVING kcals 488 • fat 9g • saturates 1g • carbs 78g • sugars 11g • fibre 12g • protein 16g • salt 1.4g

Mexican bean soup with shredded chicken and lime

Use leftover chicken breast in this substantial healthy soup. Alternatively, make the recipe vegetarian by topping with chunky, fresh guacamole.

 TAKES 5 hours ⏻ SERVES 2

- 2 tsp rapeseed oil
- 1 large onion, finely chopped
- 1 red pepper, cut into chunks
- 2 garlic cloves, chopped
- 2 tsp mild chilli powder
- 1 tsp ground coriander
- 1 tsp ground cumin
- 400g can chopped tomatoes
- 400g can black beans
- 1 tsp vegetable bouillon powder
- 1 cooked skinless chicken breast (about 125g), shredded
- handful chopped coriander
- 1 lime, juiced
- ½ red chilli, deseeded and finely chopped (optional)

1 Heat the slow cooker if necessary. Heat the oil in a frying pan, add the onion and pepper, and fry, stirring frequently, for 10 mins. Stir in the garlic and spices, then tip into the slow cooker. Pour in the tomatoes and half a can of water and the bouillon powder. Cook on Low for 4 hours. Stir in the beans and cook for a further 30 mins.

2 When you are ready to serve, tip the chicken into a bowl, add the coriander and lime juice with a little chilli and toss well. Ladle the soup into 2 bowls, top with the chicken and serve.

GOOD TO KNOW healthy
PER SERVING kcals 378 • fat 8g • saturates 1g • carbs 36g • sugars 17g • fibre 12g • protein 32g • salt 0.5g

Moroccan harira

This is a healthy vegetarian version of the classic Moroccan soup with plenty of turmeric and cinnamon, each offering different health benefis, plus it's low in fat and calories too.

 TAKES 4½ hours SERVES 4

- 1–2 tbsp rapeseed oil
- 2 large onions, finely chopped
- 4 garlic cloves, chopped
- 2 tsp turmeric
- 2 tsp ground cumin
- ½ tsp ground cinnamon
- 2 red chillies, deseeded and sliced
- 500g carton passata
- 800ml low-salt vegetable bouillon
- 175g dried green lentils
- 2 carrots, chopped into small pieces
- 1 sweet potato, peeled and diced
- 5 celery sticks, chopped into small pieces
- ⅔ small pack coriander, few sprigs reserved, the rest chopped
- 1 lemon, cut into 4 wedges, to serve

1 Heat the slow cooker if necessary. Heat the oil in a large non-stick sauté pan over a medium heat and fry the onions and garlic until starting to soften. Tip in the spices and chilli, stir briefly, then scoop everything into the slow cooker. Pour in the passata and stock. Add the lentils, carrots, sweet potato and celery, and cook on Low for 4 hours.

2 Stir in the chopped coriander and serve in bowls with lemon wedges for squeezing over, and the reserved coriander sprinkled over.

GOOD TO KNOW healthy • vegetarian • low-fat
PER SERVING kcals 335 • Fat 6g • Saturates 1g • Carbs 48g • Sugars 21g • Fibre 13g • Protein 16g • Salt 0.2g

Bone broth

This immune-supportive soup, made from bones and flavoured with bay, lemon and herbs, is packed with nutrients for healthy bones, hair and nails. Ask your butcher to cut the bones into short lengths if they are big or you want to be able to fit them in your slow cooker.

🕐 TAKES 18-36 hours 🕐 SERVES 4

- Beef, veal bones and or chicken, ask your butcher what he has
- 2 carrots, roughly chopped
- 1 leek, roughly chopped
- 1 celery stick, roughly chopped
- juice 1 lemon
- 1 bay leaf

1 Heat oven to 180C/160C fan/gas 4. Spread the bones out on a baking sheet and roast them for an hour, turning them over after 30 mins.

2 Heat the slow cooker if necessary. Pack the veg into the slow cooker, add the bones and enough water to fill the pot to within 2cm of the top. Add the lemon juice and the bay leaves. Cover and cook on Low for 18–36 hours. The longer your cook the broth for the darker it will become.

3 Place a colander over a bowl and scoop out all the bones into the colander. Return any broth from the bowl to the pan. Strain all the liquid through a fine sieve. Taste, and season only if you need to. Allow the broth to cool and lift off the fat. Store in the fridge for up to 3 days or transfer to freezer bags once it has cooled.

GOOD TO KNOW gluten-free • low-fat • healthy
NUTRITION (per serving) kcals 45 • fat 0.3g • saturates 0.1g • carbs 4g • sugars 2g • fibre 0.2g • protein 6g • salt 0.65g

Chapter 3:

FAMILY FAVOURITES

· ·

Make the most of busy weeknights with our family-friendly slow cooker dinners. We've got dishes to suit all ages and tastes, from shepherd's pie to a creamy chicken korma (that's low-calorie and low-fat to boot). We've got casseroles and stews for all the seasons, from a warming beef and swede casserole to a simple spring chicken in a pot. Plus, say goodbye to expensive takeaways – you can have your curry and eat it with our super healthy, Indian-inspired dishes. Kids will love the fruity flavour and mild spices of our creamy chicken and mango curry, while chilli fans can turn up the heat on our healthier chicken balti. The only question left - who's turn is it to do the washing up?

Big-batch Bolognese

Don't worry if your slow cooker is too small for this recipe, it is really easy to reduce the quantities, and it will taste delicious no matter how much you make.

 TAKES 9½ hours · SERVES 12

- 4 tbsp olive oil
- 6 rashers smoked bacon, chopped
- 1.5kg lean mince beef
- 4 onions, finely chopped
- 3 carrots, finely chopped
- 4 celery sticks, finely chopped
- 500g mushrooms, sliced
- 8 garlic cloves, crushed
- 2 tbsp dried mixed herbs
- 2 bay leaves
- 4 x 400g cans chopped tomatoes
- 6 tbsp tomato purée
- 4 tbsp red wine vinegar
- 1 tbsp caster sugar
- pasta, to serve
- Parmesan shavings, to garnish

1 Heat the slow cooker if necessary. Heat the oil in a very large pan and fry the bacon and mince, in batches, until browned. Tip into the slow cooker and stir in the vegetables, garlic, herbs, chopped tomatoes, purée, vinegar and sugar with some seasoning.

2 Cover and cook on Low for 6–8 hours, then uncover, turn to High and cook for another hour until thick and saucy, and the mince is tender. Serve with pasta and scattered shavings of Parmesan.

GOOD TO KNOW healthy
PER SERVING kcals 321 · fat 19g · saturates 7g · carbs 8g · sugars 7g · fibre 2g · protein 31g · salt 1.27g

Chicken arrabbiata

The name actually means 'angry' – and just like the pasta sauce, this dish is intended to pack quite a punch.

 TAKES 9½ hours SERVES 4

- 350ml red wine
- 3 tbsp olive oil
- 2 medium onions, halved and sliced
- 1 garlic bulb, separated into cloves
- 2 red chillies, deseeded and sliced
- 150ml chicken stock
- 600g tomatoes, finely chopped
- 3 tbsp tomato purée
- 2 tsp chopped thyme leaves
- 6 chicken legs, skin removed
- chopped parsley, to garnish (optional)
- pasta or mashed potato, to serve

1 Heat the slow cooker if necessary. Put the wine in a small pan and bring to a simmer. Let it bubble for a minute then pour it into the slow cooker pot and stir in the olive oil, onions, garlic cloves, chillies, stock, tomatoes, tomato purée and thyme with some seasoning. Add the chicken legs, pushing them under the liquid, then cook on Low for 8–9 hours until the chicken is tender.

2 Serve scattered with parsley, if you like, and pasta or mashed potato.

GOOD TO KNOW healthy
PER SERVING kcals 327 • fat 13g • saturates 3g • carbs 9g • sugars 7g • fibre 3g • protein 35g • salt 0.5g

Light chicken korma

This curry is low-fat and low-calorie, so there's no excuse not to make it right away and tuck in!

TAKES 3 hours   SERVES 4

- 1 onion, chopped
- 2 garlic cloves, roughly chopped
- thumb-sized piece ginger, roughly chopped
- 4 tbsp korma paste
- 50g ground almonds
- 4 tbsp sultanas
- 250ml chicken stock
- ¼ tsp golden caster sugar
- 4 boneless chicken breasts, skin removed
- 150g pot fat-free Greek yogurt
- small bunch coriander, chopped
- few flaked almonds, to scatter (optional)
- basmati rice, to serve

1 Heat the slow cooker if necessary. Put the onion, garlic and ginger in a food processor and whizz to a paste. Scrape the paste into the slow cooker pot and mix with the korma paste, ground almonds, sultanas, chicken stock and sugar. Push in the chicken breasts, cover and cook on High for 2 hours until the chicken is cooked through and tender.

2 Fish out the chicken breasts and dice into chunks. Stir back into the sauce. Cover and cook for 20–30 mins more on High, just to heat through.

3 Remove from the heat, stir in the yogurt and some seasoning, then scatter over the coriander and flaked almonds, if using. Serve with brown or white basmati rice.

GOOD TO KNOW healthy
PER SERVING kcals 376 • fat 11g • saturates 1g • carbs 28g • sugars 26g • fibre 3g • protein 40g • salt 1.1g

Beef and swede casserole

This gluten and dairy free casserole is hearty and comforting, packed with chunky meat and veg. Simple to prepare, serve up with seasonal greens.

 TAKES 10½ hours SERVES 4

- 2 tbsp vegetable oil
- 2 onions, sliced
- ½ celery stick, sliced
- 500g diced braising beef
- 100ml red wine (optional)
- 300ml beef stock (or chicken)
- 500g swede, peeled and cut into chunky dice
- 300g floury potatoes (such as Maris Piper), diced
- 3 thyme sprigs
- 1 bay leaf
- green vegetables, to serve (optional)

1 Heat the slow cooker if necessary. Heat the oil in a frying pan over a medium-high heat. Fry the onions and celery for a few mins until turning brown. Add the beef and brown all over for 3–4 mins. Pour in the wine, if using, and let it reduce by half. Add the stock and bring back to a boil, tip into the slow cooker. Toss in the swede, potatoes, thyme and bay leaf. Season and cook on Low for 6–8 hours.

2 If you want to reduce the liquid a little, remove the lid, turn up the heat to high and cook until the sauce has thickened a little. Season to taste and remove the thyme sprigs and bay leaf. Serve with some green veg, if you like.

GOOD TO KNOW healthy • gluten-free
PER SERVING kcals 352 • fat 15g • saturates 4g • carbs 20g • sugars 7g • fibre 5g • protein 30g • salt 0.6g

Spicy root and lentil casserole

The potatoes in this recipe take on the spicy flavours beautifully – our idea of the perfect veggie supper.

 TAKES 8½ hours 35 mins SERVES 4

- 2 tbsp sunflower or vegetable oil
- 1 onion, chopped
- 2 garlic cloves, crushed
- 700g potatoes, peeled and cut into chunks
- 4 carrots, thickly sliced
- 2 parsnips, thickly sliced
- 2 tbsp curry paste or powder
- 1 litre vegetable stock
- 100g red lentils
- a small bunch coriander, roughly chopped
- low-fat yogurt and naan bread, to serve

1 Heat the slow cooker if necessary. Heat the oil in a large pan and cook the onion and garlic over a medium heat for 3–4 mins until softened, stirring occasionally. Tip in the potatoes, carrots and parsnips, turn up the heat and cook for 6–7 mins, stirring, until the vegetables are golden.

2 Stir in the curry paste or powder and cook for a minute, then transfer to the slow cooker. Cook on Low for 4 hours. Bring the stock to the boil and pour into the slow cooker. Add the lentils, cover and cook on Low 4 hours until the lentils and vegetables are tender. Mash some of the vegetables lightly to thicken the sauce.

3 Stir in most of the coriander, season and heat for a minute or so. Top with yogurt and the rest of the coriander. Serve with naan bread.

GOOD TO KNOW vegetarian • healthy
PER SERVING kcals 378 • fat 9g • saturates 1g • carbs 64g • sugars 0g • fibre 10g • protein 14g • salt 1.24g

Smoky pork and Boston beans one-pot

You can use skinless chicken thighs on the bone instead of pork if you prefer. They will take the same time to cook.

 TAKES 4½ hours SERVES 4

- 2 tbsp olive oil
- 2 garlic cloves, crushed
- 2 tbsp smoked paprika
- 500g pork shoulder steaks, all fat trimmed and quartered
- 500g carton passata
- 2 x 400g cans cannellini beans, drained
- 1–2 tsp chipotle paste
- 1 tbsp dark soft brown sugar
- 1 tbsp red wine vinegar
- 1 low-salt chicken stock cube
- 75g ham hock, in large shreds
- 4 slices crusty white bread
- small handful flat-leaf parsley, roughly chopped

1 Heat the slow cooker if necessary. Mix the oil, garlic and paprika together and rub into the pork. Heat a non-stick frying pan and seal the pork on both sides then lift from the pan.
2 Pour in the passata, cannellini beans, chipotle, sugar, vinegar, crumbled stock cube and ham hock and heat until bubbling. Tip into the slow cooker pot and nestle the pork into the beans. Cover and cook on Low for 4 hours until the pork is tender.
3 Toast the bread and serve on the side. Sprinkle the parsley over the pork and beans to serve.

GOOD TO KNOW 2 of 5 a day • low-calorie • healthy
PER SERVING kcals 472 • fat 14g • saturates 3g • carbs 37g • sugars 13g • fibre 11g • protein 43g
• salt 1.22g

Easy one-pot chicken

This make a very quick and easy family meal in one. Serve with a knife, fork and spoon for the sauce, or mash the potatoes into the sauce as you eat it.

TAKES 4½ hours · SERVES 4

- 8 bone-in chicken thighs, skin removed
- 1 tbsp sunflower oil
- 2 large carrots, cut into batons
- 400g new potatoes, halved if large
- 5 spring onions, sliced, white and green parts kept separate
- 2 tbsp plain flour
- 1 low-salt chicken stock cube
- 1 tbsp grainy or Dijon mustard
- 200g frozen peas
- small pack fresh soft herbs, like parsley, chives or tarragon, chopped (optional)

1 Heat the slow cooker if necessary. Put the kettle on. Fry the thighs in the oil in a large non-stick frying pan to brown them. Put them in the slow cooker pot with the carrots and potatoes.

2 Stir the whites of the spring onion into the chicken pan juices with the flour, crumble in the stock cube and stir for 1–2 mins. Gradually stir in 600ml hot water from the kettle, bring the boil, stirring, then pour into the slow cooker pot. Stir to mix, then cover and cook on Low for 3½ hours.

3 Take off the lid and quickly stir in the mustard, peas and spring onion tops, then cover and cook for 40 mins more. Add the herbs, if using, and some seasoning to taste before serving.

GOOD TO KNOW 1 of 5 a day • low-calorie • low-fat • healthy • high in fibre
PER SERVING kcals 381 • fat 12g • saturates 3g • carbs 33g • sugars 8g • fibre 8g • protein 30g • salt 0.95g

Minced beef and sweet potato stew

You can make this with lamb mince too if you like, or even half lamb mince, half beef mince if you've got bits to use up.

 TAKES 9 hours SERVES 4

- 1 tbsp sunflower oil
- 500g lean mince beef
- 1 large onion, chopped
- 1 large carrot, chopped
- 1 celery stick, sliced
- 1 tbsp each tomato purée and mushroom ketchup
- 400g can chopped tomatoes
- 350g sweet potatoes, peeled and cut into large chunks
- few thyme sprigs
- 1 bay leaf
- handful parsley, chopped
- shredded and steamed Savoy cabbage, to serve

1 Heat your slow cooker if necessary. Heat the oil in a large frying pan, add the beef and cook until it is browne dall over.
2 Put the mince in your slow cooker pot with the onion, carrot, celery, tomato purée, mushroom ketchup, chopped tomatoes, sweet potatoes, thyme, bay leaf and 200ml water. Season, cover and then cook on Low for 6–8 hours until the mince and potatoes are tender.
3 Once cooked, remove the bay leaf, stir through the chopped parsley and serve with the shredded and steamed cabbage.

GOOD TO KNOW 3 of 5 a day • low-calorie • healthy • high in fibre
PER SERVING kcals 359 • fat 15g • saturates 5g • carbs 25g • sugars 15g • fibre 6g • protein 28g • salt 1g

Mumbai Potato Wraps with Minted Yogurt relish

These spicy potatoes are fantastic in indian-style wraps, but you can just as easily spoon them over rice, or serve in bowls with a wedge of naan bread to dunk in.

 TAKES 3¼ hours SERVES 4

- 1 onion, sliced
- 2 tbsp medium curry powder
- 400g can chopped tomatoes
- 750g potatoes, diced
- 2 tbsp mango chutney, plus extra to taste (optional)
- 100g low-fat natural yogurt
- 1 tsp mint sauce from a jar
- 8 small plain chapatis
- small bunch coriander, to garnish

1 Heat the slow cooker if necessary. Tip the onion, curry powder, chopped tomatoes, potatoes and mango chutney into the slow cooker pot with 50ml boiling water. Stir everything together, then cover and cook for 3 hours on High until the potatoes are tender. Season.

2 Meanwhile, mix together the yogurt and mint sauce, and warm the chapatis following the pack instructions.

3 To serve, spoon some of the potatoes on to a chapatis and top with a few sprigs of coriander. Drizzle with the minted yogurt relish, adding extra mango chutney, if you wish, then roll up and eat.

GOOD TO KNOW 2 of 5 a day • low-calorie (as a main) • healthy • high in fibre • vegetarian • low-fat
PER SERVING kcals 485 • fat 7g • saturates 3g • carbs 87g • sugars 14g • fibre 9g • protein 13g • salt 1.12g

Spring chicken in a pot

Casseroles aren't just for winter – this light, vibrant one-pot is packed with spring veg and herby pesto. This recipe needs a 5 litre slow cooker but can be easily halved.

TAKES 5 hours SERVES 4

- 1 tbsp olive oil
- 1 onion, chopped
- 500g boneless, skinless chicken thighs
- 300g small new potatoes
- 200ml low-salt vegetable stock
- 350g broccoli, cut into small florets
- 250g spring greens, shredded
- 140g petits pois
- bunch spring onions, sliced
- 2 tbsp pesto

1 Heat the slow cooker if necessary. Heat the oil in a large frying pan. Add the onion, gently fry for 5 mins until softened, add the chicken, then fry until lightly coloured. Tip into the slow cooker. Heat the stock to boiling. Add the potatoes, stock and plenty of freshly ground black pepper. Cover, then cook on Low for 4 hours until the potatoes are tender and the chicken is cooked. Can be frozen at this point.

2 Add the broccoli, spring greens, petits pois and spring onions, stir well, then return to the boil. Cover, then cook for 30 mins more, stir in the pesto and heat through.

GOOD TO KNOW healthy
PER SERVING kcals 339 • fat 10g • saturates 3g • carbs 27g • sugars 12g • fibre 8g • protein 36g • salt 0.5g

Moroccan chicken one-pot

You don't need a clay pot to whip up a fragrant, North Africa tagine – throw it all in a slow cooker and top with feta, mint and lemon.

🕐 TAKES 5 hours 🕒 SERVES 6

- 4 boneless, skinless chicken breasts
- 3 tbsp olive oil
- 2 onions, 1 roughly chopped, 1 sliced
- 100g tomatoes, chopped
- 100g ginger, roughly chopped
- 3 garlic cloves
- 1 tsp turmeric
- 1 tbsp each ground cumin, coriander and cinnamon
- 1 large butternut squash, deseeded and cut into big chunks
- 300ml chicken stock, brought to a boil
- 2 tbsp brown sugar
- 2 tbsp red wine vinegar
- 100g dried cherries

TO SERVE
- 1 small red onion, finely chopped
- zest 1 lemon
- handful mint leaves
- 100g feta crumbled
- couscous and natural yogurt

1 Heat the slow cooker if necessary. Season the chicken. Heat 2 tbsp of the oil in a flameproof dish, then brown the chicken on all sides. Transfer the chicken to the slow cooker. Whizz the chopped onion, tomatoes, ginger and garlic into a rough paste. Fry the sliced onion in the remaining oil in the dish until softened, then add the spices and fry for 1 min more until fragrant. Add the paste and fry for another few mins to soften, then add to the chicken.

2 Add the squash, stock, sugar and vinegar. Cook on Low for 4 hours. Lift the chicken out and stir in the cherries, then continue to cook on high for 30 mins while you shred the chicken into bite-sized chunks. Stir the chicken back into the sauce and season.

3 Mix the red onion, lemon zest, mint and feta. Scatter over the dish, then serve with some couscous and yogurt.

GOOD TO KNOW healthy
PER SERVING kcals 324 • fat 7g • saturates 1g • carbs 39g • sugars 24g • fibre 6g
• protein 27g • salt 0.4g

Chicken and white bean stew

This flavoursome, low-fat casserole freezes really well, so if you have a very large slow cooker why not make double and freeze half for next time.

🕐 TAKES 5 hours 🕐 SERVES 4

- 2 tbsp sunflower oil
- 400g boneless, skinless chicken thighs, trimmed and cut into chunks
- 1 onion, finely chopped
- 3 carrots, finely chopped
- 3 celery sticks, finely chopped
- 2 thyme sprigs or ½ tsp dried
- 1 bay leaf, fresh or dried
- 300ml vegetable or chicken stock, brought to a boil
- 2 x 400g cans haricot beans, drained
- chopped parsley, to serve

1 Heat the slow cooker if necessary. Heat the oil in a large frying pan, add the chicken, then fry until lightly browned and transfer to the slow cooker. Add the veg to the frying pan, then fry for a few mins more and transfer to the slow cooker. Stir in the herbs and stock, stir well, reduce the heat, then cover and cook on Low for 4 hours, until the chicken is tender.
2 Stir the beans into the stew, then cook for 30 mins. Stir in the parsley and serve with crusty bread.

GOOD TO KNOW gluten-free • healthy
PER SERVING kcals 291 • fat 9g • saturates 2g • carbs 24g • sugars 9g • fibre 11g • protein 30g • salt 0.66g

One-pot lentil chicken

This all-in-one meal makes a brilliant guilt-free supper, and if you are really hungry – just add potatoes.

🕐 TAKES 4½ hours 🕐 SERVES 2

- 1 tsp vegetable oil
- 2 rashers lean dry-cure back bacon, trimmed and chopped
- 2 large bone-in chicken thighs, skin removed
- 1 medium onion, thinly sliced
- 1 garlic clove, thinly sliced
- 2 tsp plain flour
- 2 tsp tomato purée
- 75ml dry white wine
- 100ml chicken stock
- 50g green lentils
- ½ tsp dried thyme
- 85g chestnut mushrooms, halved if large

1 Heat the slow cooker if necessary. Heat the oil in a non-stick wide, shallow pan, add the bacon and fry briskly until lightly coloured, then lift into the slow cooker. Add the chicken and fry on each side until lightly brown. Add to the bacon. Tip onion and garlic into the pan and cook for 5 mins. Stir in the flour and tomato purée, then stir over a low heat for 2–3 mins. Add the wine, stock, lentils and thyme. Bring to the boil and tip into the slow cooker. Stir in the mushrooms.

2 Cover and cook on Low for 4 hours, or until lentils are tender and the chicken cooked. Season with salt and pepper.

GOOD TO KNOW healthy
PER SERVING *kcals 360 • fat 10g • saturates 3g • carbs 14g • sugars 0g • fibre 2.5g • protein 41g • salt 2.4g*

Paprika pork

This super healthy pork one-pot is a midweek miracle. Serve with rice or noodles for an everyday favourite.

🕐 TAKES 4½ hours 🕐 SERVES 4

- 1 tbsp olive oil
- 2 onions, finely sliced
- 400g pork fillet, trimmed of any fat, cut into thick strips
- 250g pack mushrooms, sliced
- 1½ tbsp sweet smoked paprika
- 1 tbsp tomato purée
- 100ml chicken stock
- 100ml soured cream
- egg noodles, tagliatelle or rice, to serve

1 Heat the slow cooker if necessary. Heat the oil in a large frying pan, tip in the onions and cook for 10 mins until soft and golden. Add the pork and mushrooms and cook on a high heat for 3–4 mins until browned. Add the paprika and cook for 1 min more, then tip into the slow cooker. Stir in the tomato purée, then pour on the stock, cover and cook on Low for 4 hours until the pork is cooked through.

2 Mix in the soured cream and some seasoning. Serve with egg noodles, tagliatelle or rice, and an extra dollop of soured cream, if you like.

GOOD TO KNOW healthy
PER SERVING) kcals 257 • fat 13g • saturates 5g • carbs 9g • sugars 5g • fibre 2g • protein 27g • salt 0.35g

Somerset stew

This family winter warmer is full of flavour and goodness, serve with herby mash if you like. This also makes a good dish to serve with grilled meat.

 TAKES 5½ hours SERVES 4

- 1 tbsp oil
- 1 onion, finely chopped
- 1 garlic clove, finely chopped
- 1 large carrot, finely chopped
- 1 leek, chopped
- 1 tbsp tomato purée
- 400g can chopped tomatoes
- 200g can butter beans, drained
- 400g can flageolet beans, rinsed and drained
- 100ml dry cider
- 100ml vegetable stock
- few sprigs thyme, leaves only

Heat the slow cooker if necessary. Heat oil in a large frying pan and fry the onion, garlic, carrot and leek until soft but not coloured, then tip into the slow cooker. Add the tomato purée, chopped tomatoes, butter beans, flageolet beans, cider, stock and thyme. Cover and cook on Low for 4–5 hours until the veg are tender.

GOOD TO KNOW vegetarian • healthy
PER SERVING (without mash) kcals 169 • fat 4g • saturates 0g • carbs 24g • sugars 10g • fibre 7g • protein 9g • salt 0.99g

Indian butternut squash curry

Get all of your 5-a-day in one hit, with this fragrant, low-fat, vegetarian curry.

 TAKES 5 hours ⟨ SERVES 4

- 1 tbsp olive oil
- 1 butternut squash, diced
- 1 red onion, diced
- 2 tbsp mild curry paste
- 150ml vegetable stock
- 4 large tomatoes, roughly chopped
- 400g can chickpeas, rinsed and drained
- 3 tbsp fat-free Greek yogurt
- small handful coriander, chopped
- 200g brown basmati rice, cooked

1 Heat the slow cooker if necessary. Heat the oil in a large frying pan and cook the butternut squash for 2–3 mins until lightly browned. Add the onion and the curry paste and fry for 3–4 mins more. Tip into the slow cooker.
2 Pour over the stock, then cover and cook on Low for 4 hours, or until the squash is tender. Add the tomatoes and chickpeas, then cook for another 30 mins, until the tomatoes slightly soften.
3 Take off the heat and stir through the yogurt and coriander. Serve with the rice and some wholemeal chapatis if you like.

GOOD TO KNOW vegetarian • healthy
PER SERVING kcals 393 • fat 8g • saturates 1g • carbs 71g • sugars 16g • fibre 9g • protein 14g • salt 0.94g

Healthier chicken balti

A lighter version of the Indian takeaway classic, this tomato-based curry is packed with extra spinach and peppers.

TAKES 4¾ hours SERVES 4 Can be frozen

- 450g skinless, boneless chicken breast, cut into bite-sized pieces
- 1 tbsp lime juice
- 1 tsp paprika
- ¼ tsp hot chilli powder
- 1½ tbsp sunflower or groundnut oil
- 1 cinnamon stick
- 3 cardamom pods, split
- 1 small to medium green chilli
- ½ tsp cumin seeds
- 1 medium onion, coarsely grated
- 2 garlic cloves, very finely chopped
- 2½cm-piece ginger, grated
- ½ tsp turmeric
- 1 tsp ground cumin
- 1 tsp ground coriander
- 1 tsp garam masala
- 250ml passata
- 1 red pepper, deseeded, cut into small chunks
- 1 medium tomato, chopped
- 115g baby spinach leaves
- handful fresh coriander, chopped
- chapatis or basmati rice, to serve (optional)

1 Put the chicken in a medium bowl. Mix in the lime juice, paprika, chilli powder and a grinding of black pepper, then leave to marinate for at least 15 mins, preferably a bit longer.

2 Heat the slow cooker if necessary. Heat 1 tbsp of the oil in a large frying pan. Tip in the cinnamon stick, cardamom pods, whole chilli and cumin seeds, and stir-fry briefly just to colour and release their fragrance Stir in the onion, garlic and ginger and fry over a medium-high heat for 3–4 mins until the onion starts to turn brown. Mix the turmeric, cumin, ground coriander and garam masala together. Tip into the frying pan, lower the heat to medium and cook for 2 mins, scrape into the slow cooker. Add the chicken to the slow cooker. Pour in the passata, then drop in the chunks of pepper. Cook on Low for 3½ hours.

3 Stir in the tomato, cook for 30 mins, then add the spinach and turn it over in the cooker to just wilt. Season with a little salt. Remove the cinnamon stick, chilli and cardamom pods, if you wish, before serving. Scatter with fresh coriander and serve with warm chapatis or basmati rice, if you like.

GOOD TO KNOW healthy
PER SERVING kcals 217 • fat 6.6g • saturates 1.3g • carbs 10.2g • sugars 8.2g • fibre 2.5g
• protein 30.2g • salt 0.5g

Chipotle chicken

Keep a jar of smoky chipotle chilli paste in your cupboard, to add a kick to a healthy chicken stew.

 TAKES 6½ hours · SERVES 4

- 1 onion, chopped
- 1 garlic clove, sliced
- 2 tbsp sunflower oil
- 1–2 tbsp chipotle paste
- 400g can chopped tomatoes
- 1 tbsp cider vinegar
- 8 boneless, skinless chicken thighs fillets
- small bunch coriander, chopped
- soured cream and rice, to serve

Heat the slow cooker if necessary. Fry the onion and garlic in the oil in a deep, wide frying pan until soft. Add the chipotle paste (use 1 tbsp for a mild flavour and 2 tbsp for a hotter, stronger one). Stir and cook for 1 min, then add the tomatoes and cider vinegar. Bring to a simmer and tip into the slow cooker. Add the chicken, cover and cook on Low for 6 hours. Scatter with coriander and serve with rice and soured cream.

GOOD TO KNOW healthy
PER SERVING *kcals 286 · fat 11g · saturates 3g · carbs 6g · sugars 4g · fibre 2g · protein 42g · salt 0.64g*

Creamy chicken and mango curry

Use korma paste, turmeric and black onion seeds as the base for this mild, Indian spice-pot, made creamy with coconut milk.

 TAKES 7 hours SERVES 6–8

- 12 boneless, skinless chicken thighs
- 2 tsp turmeric
- 2 tbsp sunflower oil
- 2 onions, 1 chopped, 1 quartered
- 2 large ripe mangoes
- 6 tbsp good-quality korma paste
- 100g ginger, roughly chopped
- 2 tsp ground cumin
- 1 tbsp black onion seeds (kalonji or nigella)
- 400g can light coconut milk
- 200ml chicken stock
- few coriander sprigs, basmati rice, naan bread, mango chutney, lime pickle, to serve (optional)

1 Heat the slow cooker if necessary. Toss the chicken thighs with 1 tsp of the turmeric and some salt. Heat the oil in a big frying pan or wide flameproof casserole, and brown the thighs well on both sides. Lift them into the slow cooker. Add the chopped onion and cook for 5 mins until softened and add it to the chicken.

2 Roughly cut all the flesh from one of the mangoes, scraping as much as you can from the stone. Put into a food processor with the korma paste, ginger and quartered onion. Whizz to a paste, then tip into the cooker.

3 Stir in the remaining turmeric, cumin and onion seeds followed by the coconut milk and stock. Cook on Low for 6 hours.

4 Slice the remaining mango and stir in to heat through while you shred the chicken with 2 forks. Season and serve scattered with the coriander, with basmati rice, naan bread, chutney and lime pickle, if you like.

GOOD TO KNOW healthy
PER SERVING (6) kcals 384 • fat 17g • saturates 6g • carbs 17g • sugars 14g • fibre 3g • protein 41g • salt 1.2g

Chunky chilli

Use chunks of stewing beef in your chilli con carne for a robust and filling dish. Serve with rice and coriander.

⏱ TAKES 9 hours 🥧 SERVES 4

- 1–2 tbsp olive oil, plus extra if needed
- 400g diced stewing beef
- 1 onion, finely chopped
- 2 garlic cloves, finely chopped
- 1½ tsp ground cumin
- 1–2 tbsp chipotle paste (or gluten-free alternative), depending on how spicy you like it
- 400g can kidney beans in chilli sauce
- 400g can chopped tomatoes
- 1 lime, zested and cut into wedges
- ¼ small pack coriander, leaves only
- cooked rice, to serve (optional)

1 Heat the slow cooker if necessary. Heat the oil in a large frying pan and cook the beef pieces for a few mins on each side until browned all over. Remove from the pan with a slotted spoon and transfer to the slow cooker.

2 Add the onion to the pan, with extra oil if needed, and cook until softened. Stir in the garlic, cumin and chipotle paste, and cook for 1 min, then tip into the slow cooker. Sieve the kidney beans, reserving the sauce. Add this sauce, along with the chopped tomatoes to the slow cooker. Cook on Low for 8 hours or until the beef is tender.

3 Add the reserved kidney beans and lime zest and cook for 30 minutes. Serve with a scattering of coriander leaves, the lime wedges to squeeze over, and rice, if you like.

GOOD TO KNOW healthy • gluten-free
PER SERVING) kcals 300 • fat 13g • saturates 3g • carbs 21g • sugars 10g • fibre 6g
• protein 26g • salt 0.9g

Lighter chicken cacciatore

The classic Italian 'hunter's stew' gets a healthy makeover, with low-fat chicken breasts, prosciutto and a rich herby tomato sauce.

🕐 TAKES 5 hours 🕑 SERVES 4

- 1 tbsp olive oil
- 3 slices prosciutto, fat removed, chopped
- 1 medium onion, chopped
- 2 garlic cloves, finely chopped
- 2 sage sprigs
- 2 rosemary sprigs
- 4 skinless chicken breasts
- 150ml dry white wine
- 400g can plum tomatoes in natural juice
- 1 tbsp tomato purée
- 225g chestnut mushrooms, quartered or halved if large
- small handful chopped flat-leaf parsley, to serve

1 Heat the slow cooker if necessary. Heat the oil in a large non-stick frying pan. Tip in the prosciutto and fry for about 2 mins until crisp. Remove with a slotted spoon, letting any fat drain back into the pan, and set aside. Put the onion, garlic and herbs in the pan and fry for 3–4 mins. Tip the onion mixture into the slow cooker, then lay the chicken breasts on top. Season with pepper. Pour the wine into the frying pan and let it bubble for 2 mins to reduce slightly, pour it into the slow cooker.

2 Add the prosciutto to the pot, then stir in the tomatoes (breaking them up with your spoon), tomato purée and mushrooms. Stir everything around a little. Cover and cook on Low for 4–4½ hours or until the chicken is cooked through. Season and scatter over the parsley to serve.

GOOD TO KNOW healthy
PER SERVING kcals 262 • fat 6.2g • saturates 1.3g • carbs 6.9g • sugars 5.2g • fibre 2.7g • protein 38.7g • salt 1g

Low-fat turkey Bolognese

Swap your usual beef mince with turkey to reduce the fat content of this classic Italian sauce and serve with wholemeal pasta.

 TAKES 6½ hours SERVES 4–6

- 400g lean mince turkey (choose breast instead of thigh mince if you can, as it has less fat)
- 2 tsp vegetable oil
- 1 large onion, chopped
- 1 large carrot, chopped
- 3 celery sticks, chopped
- 250g mushrooms chopped
- pinch sugar
- 1 tbsp tomato purée
- 2 x 400g cans chopped tomatoes with garlic and herbs
- 200ml chicken stock, made from 1 low-salt stock cube, brought to a boil
- cooked wholemeal pasta and fresh basil leaves (optional), to serve

1 Heat the slow cooker if necessary. Heat a large non-stick frying pan and dry-fry the turkey mince until browned. Tip onto a plate and set aside.

2 Add the oil and gently cook the onion, carrot and celery until softened, about 10 mins (add a splash of water if it starts to stick). Add the mushrooms and cook for a few mins, then add the sugar and tomato purée, and cook for 1 min more, stirring to stop it from sticking.

3 Tip the onion mixture into the slow cooker and add the tomatoes, turkey and stock with some seasoning. Cook on Low for 6 hours. Serve with the pasta and fresh basil, if you have it.

GOOD TO KNOW healthy
PER SERVING (4) *kcals 267 • fat 13g • saturates 3g • carbs 15g • sugars 12g • fibre 6g • protein 23g • salt 1.3g*

Easy chicken and chickpea tagine

Making a mouthwatering Moroccan-inspired meal doesn't have to be difficult – this no-fuss one-pot dinner is full of flavour.

 TAKES 5½ hours ⏲ SERVES 4

- 800g boneless, skinless chicken thighs, cut into large chunks
- 1 tbsp harissa paste
- 1 tbsp vegetable oil
- 1 large onion, finely sliced
- 1 tsp ground cinnamon
- 1 tsp ground cumin
- 1 tsp turmeric
- 250ml chicken stock
- 400g can chopped tomatoes
- 100g raisins
- 400g can chickpeas, drained and rinsed
- 250g couscous, to serve
- small handful mint, leaves only, to serve

1 Mix the chicken thighs with the harissa in a large bowl and chill, covered, for 20–30 mins.
2 Meanwhile heat the slow cooker if necessary. Heat the oil in a large frying pan and fry the chicken for 2–3 mins until browned. Remove from the pan and set aside.
3 Fry the onion for 8–10 mins until soft, then stir in the spices and tip into the slow cooker. Add the chicken, together with the stock, tomatoes and raisins. Season, then cook on Low for 4 hours.
4 Add the chickpeas, and cook for 30 mins. Serve with couscous and a handful of mint leaves on top.

GOOD TO KNOW healthy
PER SERVING *kcals 456 • fat 11g • saturates 2g • carbs 34g • sugars 23g • fibre 7g • protein 52g • salt 1.3g*

Lamb dopiaza with broccoli rice

Simple and delicious, this low-fat curry is full of good-for-you ingredients, including lean lamb, prebiotic onions and fibre-rich lentils.

🕐 TAKES 8 hours 🍳 SERVES 2

- 225g lamb leg steaks, trimmed of excess fat and cut into 2.5cm chunks
- 50g full-fat natural bio yogurt, plus 4 tbsp to serve
- 1 tbsp medium curry powder
- 2 tsp cold-pressed rapeseed oil
- 2 medium onions, 1 thinly sliced, 1 cut into 5 wedges
- 2 garlic cloves, peeled and finely sliced
- 1 tbsp ginger, peeled and finely chopped
- 1 small red chilli, finely chopped (deseeded if you don't like it too hot)
- 200g tomatoes, roughly chopped
- 50g dried split red lentils, rinsed
- ½ small pack coriander, roughly chopped, plus extra to garnish
- 100g pack baby leaf spinach

FOR THE BROCCOLI RICE
- 100g wholegrain brown rice
- 100g small broccoli florets

1 Heat the slow cooker if necessary. Put the lamb in a large bowl and season well with ground black pepper. Add the yogurt and ½ tbsp of the curry powder, and stir well to combine.

2 Heat half the oil in a large frying pan. Fry the onion wedges over a high heat for 4–5 mins or until lightly browned and just tender. Tip onto a plate, set aside and return the pan to the heat. Add the remaining oil, the sliced onions, garlic, ginger and chilli, cover and cook for 10 mins or until very soft, stirring occasionally. Remove the lid, increase the heat and cook for 2–3 mins more or until the onions are tinged with brown – this will add lots of flavour, but make sure they don't get burnt.

3 Reduce the heat once more and stir in the tomatoes and remaining curry powder. Tip into the slow cooker. Stir in the lamb and yogurt plus 150ml cold water, stir in the lentils and coriander, cover with a lid and cook on Low for 6–7 hours.

4 With half an hour of the curry cooking time remaining, cook the rice in plenty of boiling water for 25 mins or until just tender. Add the broccoli florets and cook for a further 3 mins. Drain well.

5 Remove the lid from the curry, add the reserved onion wedges and continue to cook for 30 minutes or until the lamb is tender. Just before serving, stir in the spinach, a handful at a time, and let it wilt. Serve with the yogurt, coriander and broccoli rice.

GOOD TO KNOW healthy • gluten-free
PER SERVING (curry only) kcals 319 • fat 8g • saturates 2g • carbs 39g • sugars 10g • fibre 7g • protein 19g • salt 0.2g

Chicken and lentil stew with gremolata

Spruce up a light tomato-based casserole with a generous sprinkling of parsley, lemon and garlic, also known as 'gremolata'.

 TAKES 4½ hours ⏲ SERVES 4

- 2 tbsp olive oil
- 8 chicken drumsticks, skin left on
- 2 onions, very finely chopped
- 6 tbsp red lentils
- 400g can chopped tomatoes
- 1 chicken stock cube, crumbled
- crusty bread, to serve

FOR THE GREMOLATA
- zest 1 lemon
- 1 garlic clove, finely chopped
- small handful parsley, finely chopped

1 Heat the slow cooker if necessary. Heat half the oil in a large frying pan, brown the drumsticks on all sides, then transfer to a plate.

2 Add the onions and remaining oil to the pan, and cook for 5 mins or so until soft. Put the lentils, tomatoes, 100ml boiling water and the stock cube in the slow cooker. Add the drumsticks to the cooker, and cook on Low for 4 hours, then season.

3 Meanwhile, make the gremolata. Mix the lemon zest, garlic and parsley together. Sprinkle over the cooked stew and serve with a chunk of crusty bread.

GOOD TO KNOW healthy
PER SERVING *kcals 337 • fat 15g • saturates 3g • carbs 20g • sugars 7g • fibre 4g • protein 32g • salt 1.2g*

Turkey chilli

Turkey mince is cheap and lean – flavour Mexican-style with cumin and paprika and serve in crisp baked potatoes or with rice.

 TAKES 5½ hours   SERVES 4

- 1 tbsp olive oil
- 1 onion, chopped
- 1 garlic clove, crushed
- 300g mince turkey
- 1 tbsp smoked paprika
- 1 tbsp ground cumin
- 1 tbsp cider vinegar
- 1 tbsp soft light brown sugar
- 350ml passata
- 4 baked potatoes, to serve
- reduced-fat Red Leicester, grated, to serve (optional)
- 4 spring onions, chopped, to serve (optional)

1 Heat the slow cooker if necessary. Heat the oil in a large frying pan over a medium heat. Add the onion, garlic and some seasoning, and cook for 5 mins until soft. Add the turkey mince and season again, then increase the heat and break up the mince with the back of your spoon. When it's browned, add the spices, vinegar, sugar and passata. Bring to a boil and tip into the slow cooker. Cook on Low for 4–5 hours.
2 If serving in potatoes cut a cross in the top of each and spoon in the chilli. Serve each potato sprinkled with cheese and spring onions.

GOOD TO KNOW healthy
PER SERVING *kcals 410 • fat 5g • saturates 1g • carbs 61g • sugars 13g • fibre 7g • protein 30g • salt 0.1g*

Spanish chicken stew

A healthy, hearty stew to feed the family, which you can prepare in just 10 minutes. This rustic meal is best served with chunks of crusty bread or rice.

 TAKES 6½ hours SERVES 4

- 2 tbsp olive oil
- 500g boneless, skinless chicken thighs
- 1 red pepper, cut into chunky pieces
- 1 large onion, sliced
- 2 garlic cloves, chopped
- 1 tbsp white wine vinegar
- 1 tbsp smoked paprika
- 200ml chicken stock
- large handful black olives
- 50g flaked almonds, toasted
- cooked rice or crusty bread, to serve

1 Heat the slow cooker if necessary. Heat 1 tbsp of the oil in a frying pan. Season the chicken and brown on both sides for 7–8 mins until golden, then set aside on a plate. Put the remaining 1 tbsp oil in the pan with the pepper, onion and garlic. Fry on a medium heat for 8 mins or until slightly golden. Add the vinegar and cook for 1 min, then tip into the slow cooker

2 Add the chicken to the slow cooker with the paprika and stock. Cook on Low for 6 hours until the chicken is cooked through. Add the olives and almonds, and serve with rice or crusty bread.

GOOD TO KNOW healthy
PER SERVING *kcals 329 • fat 17g • saturates 3g • carbs 8g • sugars 6g • fibre 4g • protein 34g • salt 0.7g*

Spicy meatball tagine with bulghar and chickpeas

Who knew meatballs could be 4 of your 5-a-day? This healthy tagine is full of flavour and low in fat, just make sure you choose a lean mince with 5% fat.

 TAKES 6½ hours   SERVES 4

- 2 onions, 1 quartered, 1 halved and sliced
- 500g extra-lean mince beef
- 2 tbsp tomato purée
- 2 garlic cloves
- 1 egg
- 1 tbsp chilli powder
- 2 tsp rapeseed oil
- 4 large carrots, cut into batons
- 1 tsp ground cumin
- 2 tsp ground coriander
- 400g can chopped tomatoes
- 1 lemon, zest removed with a potato peeler, then chopped
- 12 Kalamata olives, chopped
- 1 tbsp vegetable bouillon powder
- ⅓ pack fresh coriander, chopped

FOR THE BULGHAR
- 200g bulghar wheat
- 400g can chickpeas
- 2 tsp vegetable bouillon powder
- 2 tsp ground coriander

1   Heat the slow cooker if necessary. Put the quartered onion in the food processor and process to finely chop it. Add the minced beef, 1 tbsp tomato purée, the garlic, egg and chilli powder and blitz to make a smoothish paste. Divide the mixture into 26 even-sized pieces and roll into balls.

2   Heat the oil in a large frying pan and cook the meatballs for about 5–10 mins to lightly brown them. Tip from the pan onto a plate.

3   Now add the sliced onion and carrots to the pan and stir-fry briefly in the pan juices to soften them a little. Add the spices and pour in the tomatoes with ½ can of water then stir in the chopped lemon zest, remaining tomato purée, olives and bouillon powder. Transfer everything to the slow cooker. Add the meatballs to the cooker then cover and cook on Low for 6 hours until the carrots are just tender. Stir in the coriander.

4   When the tagine is almost ready, tip the bulghar into a pan with the chickpeas and water from the can. Add 2 cans of water, the bouillon and coriander. Cover and cook for 10 mins until the bulghar is tender and the liquid had been absorbed.

GOOD TO KNOW healthy
PER SERVING kcals 484 • fat 12g • saturates 3g • carbs 47g • sugars 15g • fibre 15g
• protein 40g • salt 1.1g

Lighter beef stew dumplings

We've cut the calories and fat and boosted the fibre in this comforting casserole by using a lean cut of beef and upping the vegetables.

 TAKES 9½ hours Serves 4

FOR THE STEW
- 1 tbsp rapeseed oil
- 2 medium onions, chopped
- 2 bay leaves
- 4 thyme sprigs, plus extra leaves to serve
- 550g chunks of lean braising steak
- 100ml red wine
- 1½ tbsp plain flour
- 1 tsp English mustard powder
- 230g can plum tomatoes
- 250ml vegetable bouillon
- 280g carrots, halved lengthways and sliced
- 400g piece butternut squash, deseeded, peeled and cut into 3-4cm in chunks
- 140g chestnut mushrooms, quartered or halved if large

FOR THE DUMPLINGS
- 140g self-raising flour
- ½ tsp English mustard powder
- 2 spring onions, ends trimmed, finely chopped
- 3 tbsp chopped parsley
- 2 tbsp rapeseed oil
- 100ml buttermilk

1 Heat the slow cooker if necessary. Heat the oil in a frying pan, tip in the onions, bay leaves and thyme sprigs, and fry over a medium heat for about 8 mins, stirring often, until the onions are turning golden. Raise the heat, add the steak and stir-fry briefly until it starts to lose its raw, red colour. Pour in the wine, stir to deglaze the brown sticky bits from the bottom of the pan, and let it bubble briefly. Lower the heat, sprinkle in the flour and mustard powder, and stir for 1 min. The meat should now be coated in a thick, rich sauce. Tip this into the slow cooker.

2 Mix in the tomatoes, stirring to break them down. Stir in the stock and add the carrots, squash and mushrooms, then cook on Low for 6–8 hours. Season with pepper.

3 When the stew is nearly cooked, make the dumplings. Put the flour, mustard powder, some pepper and a pinch of salt in a bowl, then stir in the spring onions and parsley. Mix the oil and buttermilk together and gently stir into the flour. Add a drop or two of cold water, if needed, to pick up any dry bits on the bottom of the bowl, and stir to make a soft and slightly sticky dough. Be as light-handed as you can, as overmixing or over handling will toughen the dumplings. Cut the dough into 8 pieces and very lightly shape each into a small, rough ball.

4 Sit the dumplings on top and press them down into the gravy to very slightly submerge. Cook on Low for 1 hour and then brown the tops gently under the grill. Serve with a light scattering of thyme leaves.

GOOD TO KNOW healthy
PER SERVING kcals 571 • fat 18g • saturates 4g • carbs 54g • sugars 18g • fibre 9g • protein 39g
• salt 0.9g

Butter bean and tomato stew

Packed full of iron, this stew makes a great side dish or a superhealthy supper when partnered with a jacket potato.

TAKES 3½ hours   Serves 5

- 3 tbsp olive oil
- 2 shallots, diced
- 2 carrots, diced
- 1 large onion, sliced
- 6 large tomatoes, chopped and sprinkled with a little salt
- 400g can butter beans, drained
- small bunch flat-leaf parsley, chopped
- harissa paste, to serve

1 Heat the slow cooker if necessary. Heat the oil in a frying pan and add the shallots, carrots and onion. Fry, stirring, until soft but not coloured then tip into the slow cooker. Add tomatoes and beans, cover and cook on Low for 2–3 hours. Taste, season, then stir in the parsley. Serve with harissa.

GOOD TO KNOW vegetarian • healthy
PER SERVING kcals 155 • fat 8g • saturates 1g • carbs 18g • sugars 11g • fibre 6g • protein 5g • salt 0.98g

Chicken gumbo

A low-fat Creole-inspired okra and green pepper stew with cayenne, paprika, cumin and thyme.

TAKES 6½ hours · SERVES 4

- 1 tbsp olive oil
- 500g boneless, skinless chicken thighs, cut into chunks
- 1 onion, chopped
- 1 green pepper, deseeded and chopped
- 3 celery sticks, finely chopped
- 1 garlic clove, finely chopped
- ¼ tsp cayenne pepper
- 1 tsp smoked paprika
- 1 tsp ground cumin
- 1 tsp dried thyme
- 1 bay leaf
- 1 heaped tbsp plain flour
- 400g can chopped tomatoes
- 200ml chicken stock, boiling
- 100g okra, cut into 2cm rounds
- small handful sage, leaves chopped
- crusty bread or microwave rice, to serve

1 Heat the slow cooker if necessary. Heat the oil in a frying pan, add the chicken and cook in batches for about 5 mins to brown all over. Remove the chicken with a slotted spoon and set aside.

2 Add the onion, green pepper and celery to the pan, put on the lid and cook for 5 mins, stirring occasionally until softened a little. Stir in the garlic, spices, thyme and bay leaf and cook for 1 min until fragrant. Tip into the slow cooker with the chicken and any juices, then stir in the flour, stirring to coat everything. Pour in the tomatoes and stock, then add the okra and half the sage. Cook on Low for 6 hours, then season and serve with bread or rice, scattering the rest of the sage over.

GOOD TO KNOW *healthy*
PER SERVING *kcals 242 · fat 7g · saturates 2g · carbs 12g · sugars 6g · fibre 4g · protein 33g · salt 0.7g*

Easy chicken tagine

This chicken tagine is great eaten with couscous for something a bit more filling.

 TAKES 6½ hours SERVES 4

- 2 tbsp olive oil
- 8 boneless, skinless chicken thighs, halved if large
- 1 onion, chopped
- 2 tsp grated ginger
- pinch saffron or tumeric
- 1 tbsp honey
- 400g carrots, cut into sticks
- small bunch parsley, roughly chopped
- lemon wedges, to serve

1 Heat the slow cooker if necessary. Heat the oil in a large, wide pan with a lid, add the chicken, then fry quickly until lightly coloured. Add the onion and ginger, then fry for a further 2 mins and tip everything into the slow cooker.

2 Add 75ml water, the saffron, honey and carrots, season, then stir well. Cover and cook on Low for 6 hours. Sprinkle with parsley and serve with lemon wedges for squeezing over.

GOOD TO KNOW healthy
PER SERVING *kcals 304 • fat 11g • saturates 3g • carbs 14g • sugars 12g • fibre 3g • protein 39g • salt 0.48g*

Classic lasagne

Mince doesn't take as long to cook as larger cuts of meat, so is ideal paired with pasta in this family classic. Make sure you go for lean mince to keep the saturated fat down, which is why we have also made the sauce without butter.

⏱ TAKES 4 ¼ hours ◔ SERVES 4

- 2 tsp rapeseed oil
- 2 onions, finely chopped
- 4 celery sticks (about 175g), finely diced
- 4 carrots (320g), finely diced
- 2 garlic cloves, chopped
- 400g lean (5% fat) mince beef
- 400g can chopped tomatoes
- 2 tbsp tomato purée
- 2 tsp vegetable bouillon
- 1 tbsp balsamic vinegar
- 1 tbsp fresh thyme leaves
- 6 wholewheat lasagne sheets (105g)

FOR THE SAUCE
- 400ml whole milk
- 50g wholemeal flour
- 1 bay leaf
- generous grating of nutmeg
- 15g finely grated Parmesan

1 Heat the slow cooker if necessary. Heat the oil in a large non-stick pan and fry the onions, celery, carrots and garlic for 5–10 mins, stirring frequently until softened and starting to colour. Tip in the meat and break it down with a wooden spoon, stirring until it browns. Pour in the tomatoes with a quarter of a can of water, the tomato purée, bouillon, balsamic vinegar, thyme and plenty of black pepper, return to the boil and cook 5 mins more.

2 Spoon half the mince in the slow cooker and top with half the lasagne, breaking it where necessary so it covers as much of the meat layer as possible. Top with the rest of the meat, and then another layer of the lasagne. Cover and cook on Low while you make the sauce.

3 Tip the milk and flour into a pan with the bay leaf and nutmeg and cook on the hob, whisking continuously until thickened. Carry on cooking for a few mins to cook the flour. Remove the bay leaf and stir in the cheese. Pour onto the pasta and spread out with a spatula then cover and cook for 3 hours until the meat is cooked and the pasta is tender. Allow to settle for 10 mins before serving with salad.

GOOD TO KNOW healthy • 3 of 5 a day • low-fat • low-calorie • high in calcium and fibre
PER SERVING kcals 448 • fat 12g • saturates 6g • carbs 46g • sugars 19g • fibre 9g • protein 33g
• salt 0.71g

Shepherd's pie

We've added sweet potatoes to our pie topping and for good reason – they contribute twice the fibre of regular potatoes, plus count towards your 5 a day!

TAKES 6 hours   SERVES 4

- 1 tbsp olive oil
- 1 onion, finely chopped
- 3–4 thyme sprigs
- 2 carrots, finely diced
- 250g lean (10% fat) mince lamb or beef
- 1 tbsp plain flour
- 1 tbsp tomato purée
- 400g can lentils or white beans
- 1 tsp Worcestershire sauce

FOR THE TOPPING
- 650g potatoes, peeled and cut into chunks
- 250g sweet potatoes, peeled and cut into chunks
- 2 tbsp half-fat crème fraiche

1 Heat the slow cooker if necessary. Heat the oil in a large frying pan. Tip in the onion and thyme sprigs and fry for 2–3 mins. Then add the carrots and fry together, stirring occasionally until the vegetables start to brown. Stir in the mince and fry for 1–2 mins until no longer pink. Stir in the flour then cook for another 1–2 mins. Stir in the tomato purée and lentils and season with pepper and the Worcestershire sauce, adding a splash of water if you think the mixture is too dry. Scrape everything into the slow cooker.

2 Meanwhile cook both lots of potatoes in simmering water for 12–15 minutes or until they are cooked through. Drain well and then mash with the crème fraiche. Spoon this on top of the mince mixture and cook on Low for 5 hours – the mixture should be bubbling at the sides when it is ready. Crisp up the potato topping under the grill if you like.

GOOD TO KNOW 3 of 5 a day • low-calorie • low-fat • healthy • high in fibre
PER SERVING kcals 438 • fat 10g • saturates 4g • carbs 57g • sugars 12g • fibre 11g • protein 23g
• salt 0.39g

Slow cooker meatballs

Turkey mince makes lighter meatballs that kids love. They also freeze well if you want to batch them up for later.

 TAKES 6 hours ⏱ SERVES 4–5

- 1 tbsp rapeseed oil
- 1 onion, finely chopped
- 2 carrots, finely diced
- 2 celery sticks, finely diced
- 2 garlic cloves, thinly sliced
- 500g carton tomato passata
- 2 tbsp chopped parsley

FOR THE MEATBALLS
- 400g lean mince turkey
- 4 tbsp porridge oats
- pinch paprika
- 1 garlic clove, crushed
- spray of oil

1 Heat the slow cooker if necessary. Heat the oil in a non-stick frying pan and add the onion, carrots, celery and garlic and fry gently for a minute. Pour in the passata, add the parsley and stir, then transfer the lot to the slow cooker.

2 To make the meatballs, tip the mince into a large bowl. Add the oats, paprika, garlic and plenty of black pepper, and mix everything together with your hands. Divide the mixture into 20 lumps about the size of a walnut and roll each piece into a meatball. Spray or rub a non-stick pan with a little oil and gently cook the meatballs until they start to brown. Add them to the tomato base and cook on Low for 5 hours. Serve over rice or pasta if you like, or with a green salad.

GOOD TO KNOW 2 of 5 a day • low-fat • healthy
PER SERVING kcals 260 • fat 5g • saturates 1g • carbs 21g • sugars 10g • fibre 5g • protein 29g • salt 0.21g

Chapter 4:

FAMILY FEASTS AND ENTERTAINING

Slow cooker fans will know that it's the perfect appliance for feeding a crowd, but if you want to give them something that's as healthy as it is delicious, you've come to the right place. We have some inventively different ideas for fuss-free entertaining, like a rich Venetian duck ragu or a fragrantly spiced beetroot and beef curry. Thought you couldn't cook fish in a slow cooker?

Think again. Our rich paprika seafood bowl and sea bass and seafood Italian one-pot put fish centre stage. If the family is clamouring for a classic Sunday roast, our potroast beef with French onion gravy is ideal, whereas hungry sports fans will appreciate a pre-game platter of Mexican pulled chicken and beans to share during the match.

Venetian duck ragu

Cinnamon adds complexity to this slow-cooked pasta sauce, which goes perfectly with large tubular paccheri pasta, or ribbons of parpadelle. Four duck legs will serve 6.

TAKES 7 hours   SERVES 6

- 1 tbsp olive oil
- 4 duck legs
- 2 onions, finely chopped
- 2 fat garlic cloves, crushed
- 2 tsp ground cinnamon
- 2 tsp plain flour
- 250ml red wine
- 2 x 400g cans chopped tomatoes
- 1 chicken stock cube, made up to 250ml chicken stock
- 3 rosemary sprigs, leaves picked and chopped
- 2 bay leaves
- 1 tsp caster sugar
- 2 tbsp milk
- 600g paccheri or pappardelle pasta
- grated Parmesan, to serve

1 Heat the slow cooker if necessary. Heat the oil in a large pan. Add the duck legs and brown on all sides for about 10 mins. Put in the slow cooker pot. Add the onions to the pan and cook for 5 mins until softened. Add the garlic and cook for a further 1 min, then stir in the cinnamon and flour and cook for a further min. Add the wine, tomatoes, stock, herbs, sugar and seasoning. Bring to a simmer, then pour into the pot, cover and cook on Low for 5–6 hours.

2 Carefully lift the duck legs out of the sauce and place on a plate – they will be very tender so try not to lose any of the meat. Pull off and discard the fat, then shred the meat with 2 forks and discard the bones. If there is a lot of excess oil on the sauce you can skim it off with a spoon. Add the meat back to the sauce with the milk and heat, uncovered, while you cook the pasta.

3 Cook the pasta following pack instructions, then drain, reserving a cup of the pasta water, and add the pasta to the ragu. Stir to coat all the pasta in the sauce, adding a splash of cooking liquid if it looks dry. Serve with grated Parmesan, if you like.

GOOD TO KNOW healthy • low-fat
PER SERVING kcals 505 • fat 12g • saturates 2g • carbs 62g • sugars 8g • fibre 2g • protein 30g • salt 0.9g

Rich paprika seafood bowl

Eating healthy isn't all about salad, this fish stew counts as 3 of your 5-a-day and it's low fat.

🕐 TAKES 11½ hours 🍷 SERVES 4

- large bunch flat-leaf parsley, leaves and stalks separated
- 1 tbsp olive oil
- 2 onions, halved and thinly sliced
- 2 celery sticks, finely chopped
- 2–3 tsp paprika
- 200g roasted red peppers, thickly sliced
- 400g can chopped tomatoes with garlic
- few fresh mussels (optional)
- 400g white fish fillet, cut into very large chunks
- crusty bread, to serve

1 Heat the slow cooker if necessary. Put the parsley stalks, half the leaves, oil and some seasoning into a food processor, and whizz to a paste. Add this and the onions, celery, paprika, peppers and chopped tomatoes to the slow cooker pot. Give everything a good stir, then cover and cook on Low for 8–10 hours.

2 If using the mussels, nestle these into the sauce and scatter the fish on top. Re-cover, then cook on High for 30 mins– 1 hour until the fish is just flaking and the mussels have opened – discard any that stay shut. Gently stir the seafood into the sauce, season, then serve in bowls with the crusty bread and a scattering of the remaining parsley.

GOOD TO KNOW healthy • 3 of 5 a day
PER SERVING kcals 192 • fat 7g • saturates 1g • carbs 12g • sugars 8g • fibre 4g • protein 22g • salt 1.14g

Salsa chicken peppers

A low-fat filler that can be warmed up easily for lunch the next day. Experiment with your favourite fillings.

🕐 TAKES 3 hours 🕐 SERVES 4

- 140g Camargue red rice or brown basmati rice
- 4 large red peppers
- oil, for brushing
- 270g jar hot salsa
- 200g cooked chicken, chopped
- 215g can red kidney beans, drained and rinsed
- 40g mature cheddar, grated
- 20g pack coriander, chopped
- lime wedges, to garnish

1 Boil the rice for 25 mins, or following the pack instructions, until just tender. Meanwhile, heat the slow cooker if necessary. Slice the tops off the peppers and cut out and discard the seeds. Set aside the peppers and their tops, then oil the base of the slow cooker pot.

2 Drain the rice and mix with the salsa, chicken, beans, cheddar and coriander. Season to taste. Fill the peppers with the rice mixture. Put on the tops, then sit the stuffed peppers in the slow cooker and cover with the lid. Cook for 2 hours on High until the peppers are tender. Squeeze over lime wedges and serve with an avocado salad.

GOOD TO KNOW 2 of 5 a day • low-calorie • healthy • high in vitamin C • folate and fibre • low-fat
PER SERVING kcals 370 • fat 10g • saturates 4g • carbs 42g • sugars 10g • fibre 10g • protein 24g • salt 1.09g

Easy paella

Whip up this traditional Spanish dish straight from the storecupboard – it's low fat too.

🕐 TAKES 3 hours 🕑 SERVES 4

- 1 tbsp olive oil
- 1 onion, chopped
- 1 tsp each hot smoked paprika and dried thyme
- 300g paella or risotto rice, rinsed until the water runs clear
- 3 tbsp dry sherry or white wine (optional)
- 400g can chopped tomatoes with garlic
- 900ml low-salt chicken stock
- 400g bag frozen mixed seafood
- juice ½ lemon, other ½ cut into wedges, to garnish
- handful flat-leaf parsley, roughly chopped, to scatter
- crusty bread, to serve

1 Heat the slow cooker if necessary. Heat the oil in a large frying pan. Add the onion and soften for 5 mins. Stir in the paprika, thyme and rice, stir for 1 min, then splash in the sherry or wine, if using. Once it has evaporated, scrape everything into the slow cooker pot. Stir in the tomatoes and stock. Season, cover and cook on High for about 2 hours.

2 Stir the frozen seafood into the pot, cover and cook for another 30 mins or until the prawns are cooked through and the rice is tender. Squeeze over the lemon juice, scatter with parsley and serve with extra lemon wedges.

GOOD TO KNOW healthy
PER SERVING kcals 431 • fat 5g • saturates 1g • carbs 66g • sugars 5g • fibre 3g • protein 34g • salt 2.14g

Chicken bacon and potato stew

Chicken casserole is even better when slow-cooked for hours so you have a delicious dish to come home to.

 TAKES 7 hours   SERVES 6

- 1 tbsp rapeseed oil
- 6 bone-in chicken thighs, skin removed
- 5 rashers smoked streaky bacon, chopped
- 200g shallots
- 350g baby new potatoes, larger ones halved
- few thyme sprigs
- 200ml white wine
- 500ml hot low-salt chicken stock
- 280ml pot buttermilk (optional)
- squeeze lemon juice
- 2 tbsp tarragon, chopped

1 Heat the slow cooker if necessary. Heat the oil in a large saucepan and brown the chicken thighs for about 10 mins, until they have a nice golden colour, then remove and set aside. Add the bacon and shallots to the pan, and brown these, too.
2 Tip everything apart from the buttermilk, lemon juice and 1 tablespoon tarragon into your slow cooker. Cover and simmer on High for 4–6 hours, until the chicken is really tender and falling off the bone.
3 Check the sauce and if you like it a little thicker, strain it into a pan and boil until thickened then return it to the pot. Stir in the buttermilk, if using. Sprinkle in the lemon juice and remaining tarragon before serving.

GOOD TO KNOW low-calorie • healthy
PER SERVING kcals 225 • fat 10g • saturates 3g • carbs 11g • sugars 3g • fibre 2g • protein 16g • salt 0.63g

Squash and venison tagine

Fragrantly spiced, this Moroccan-style stew with ginger, cinnamon and cloves will become your go-to main dish for a make ahead dinner party menu. Use a small food processor to make the spice paste.

🕐 TAKES 5 hours 🍴 SERVES 4

FOR THE SPICE PASTE
- 1 tbsp each cumin and coriander seeds
- 1 tsp black peppercorns
- 1 cinnamon stick
- 2 cloves
- bunch coriander, stalks roughly chopped, leaves picked
- thumb-sized piece ginger, peeled and roughly chopped
- 3 garlic cloves, crushed
- 1 fat red chilli, deseeded and roughly chopped

FOR THE TAGINE
- 2–3 tbsp sunflower oil
- 250g shallots, halved
- 600g butternut squash, peeled, seeds removed and cut into large pieces
- 450g stewing venison (shoulder or shin is best), cut into large pieces
- good pinch saffron
- 500ml chicken stock
- 8 pitted prunes, halved
- 2 tbsp pomegranate molasses
- bulghar, quinoa or brown rice, to serve
- yogurt, to serve

1 First make the spice paste. Heat a frying pan and tip in the cumin, coriander seeds, peppercorns, cinnamon stick and cloves. Warm the spices through, stirring them around from time to time, until they turn a shade darker and smell aromatic. Put the cinnamon stick to one side for later, and tip the remaining spices into the small bowl of a food processor. Whizz to a powder. Add the coriander stalks, ginger, garlic, chilli and 1 tsp salt, and blend to a paste with a little water.

2 Heat the slow cooker if necessary. Heat 1 tablespoon of the oil in a large pan, add the shallots and cook until starting to colour. Lift out and put in the slow cooker pot with the squash.

3 Add the remaining oil to the pan and brown the venison – you'll need to do this in batches so that you don't overcrowd the pan. Take your time, ensuring the meat has a nice dark-brown crust before you remove it from the pan – this will give the tagine a good rich flavour.

4 When all the venison pieces have been browned, return the meat to the pan with the cinnamon stick. Stir in the spice paste and sizzle for 1–2 mins, splashing in a little water if the paste starts to stick to the bottom of the pan. Add the saffron and pour in the stock. Cover and cook on Low for 3 hours.

5 Add the prunes and pomegranate with some seasoning and cook for 1 hour more. Stir through the coriander leaves and serve with your favourite grain – and a dollop of yogurt.

GOOD TO KNOW 2 of 5 a day • low-fat • healthy • high in fibre and iron
PER SERVING kcals 333 • fat 9g • saturates 2g • carbs 26g • sugars 20g • fibre 8g • protein 33g • salt 0.83g

Slow-cooked beetroot and beef curry

This Pakistani curry has a deep purple hue and is flavoured with fragrant cinnamon, cumin and coriander. Beetroot is a good source of vitamins and minerals, including folate, iron, manganese and potassium.

🕐 TAKES 4½ hours   ◔ SERVES 4

- 3–4 tbsp rapeseed oil
- 3 green cardamoms
- 2.5cm cinnamon stick
- 1 tsp each cumin and coriander seeds
- 2 medium red onions, sliced
- 1 tsp each grated garlic and ginger
- 2 medium tomatoes, chopped
- 1 tsp red chilli powder
- 450g stewing beef, cut into 2.5cm chunks
- 350g raw beetroot, grated

TO SERVE
- small pack coriander leaves
- 1 green chilli, chopped
- squeeze of ½ lime
- naan bread or basmati rice

1 Heat the slow cooker if necessary. Using a large, non-stick wok or saucepan, heat the oil over a medium flame, add the cardamom, cinnamon, cumin and coriander seeds. Once the spices start to sizzle, add the onions and stir-fry until light golden brown.

2 Add the garlic and ginger and cook for 1 min. Add a splash of water if the garlic and ginger start to stick to the pan, then add the tomatoes and cook until soft.

3 Add 1 tsp salt, chilli powder and the beef, turn up the heat and stir-fry until the meat is sealed on all sides. Stir in the beetroot and 75ml water then tip into the slow cooker pot, cover and cook on Low for 3½–4 hours until the beef is tender.

4 The finished dish should be a thick, mushy curry with chunky, tender beef pieces and softened beetroot. Sprinkle with the coriander leaves and green chilli; add a squeeze of lime, and serve with naan or basmati rice.

GOOD TO KNOW 2 of 5 a day • healthy • high in iron and folate
PER SERVING kcals 323 • fat 16g • saturates 3g • carbs 14g • sugars 12g • fibre 5g • protein 28g • salt 0.47g

Andalusian-style chicken

Spicy, sweet and fragrant, this tastes even better if you make it ahead – a centre piece for any tapas or buffet spread.

 TAKES 5½ hours ⏱ SERVES 6

- generous pinch saffron
- 1 chicken stock cube, crumbled into 300ml boiling water
- 2 tbsp olive oil
- 2 small onions, thinly sliced
- 12 bone-in chicken thighs, skin removed
- ¼ tsp ground cinnamon
- 1–2 red chillies, deseeded and chopped
- 4 tbsp sherry vinegar
- 1–2 tbsp clear honey
- 12 cherry tomatoes, quartered
- 2 tbsp raisins
- handful coriander, roughly chopped, to garnish
- 50g toasted pine nuts or almonds, to garnish

1 Heat the slow cooker if necessary. Stir the saffron into the hot stock to infuse. Heat the oil in a pan and fry the onions until soft and just beginning to turn golden. Tip into the slow cooker pot. Add the chicken to the pan and fry for a few mins until the chicken is browned all over, then add that to the pot too.

2 Stir the cinnamon and chilli into the pan, then add the stock, vinegar, honey, tomatoes and raisins and bring to the boil. Tip into the slow cooker, cover and cook on Low for 5 hours until the chicken is tender. Check the sauce and if it is a little thin, pour it from the pot and boil rapidly in a frying pan to reduce it. Pour back into the pot, scatter with the coriander and nuts, and serve.

GOOD TO KNOW *1 of 5 a day • healthy*
PER SERVING *kcals 239 • fat 12g • saturates 3g • carbs 9g • sugars 8g • fibre 1g • protein 24g • salt 0.58g*

Sea bass and seafood Italian one-pot

A one-pot fish stew with shellfish and all the fresh flavours of the Mediterranean – serve with plenty of bread for dipping.

 TAKES 4 hours SERVES 4

- 2 tbsp olive oil
- 1 fennel bulb, halved and sliced, fronds kept to garnish
- 2 garlic cloves, sliced
- ½ red chilli, deseeded and chopped
- 250g prepared squid, sliced into rings
- bunch basil, leaves and stalks separated, stalks tied together, leaves roughly torn
- 400g can chopped tomatoes
- 75ml white wine
- 2 large handfuls mussels or clams
- 8 large raw prawns
- 4 sea bass fillets (about 140g each)
- crusty bread, to serve

1 Heat the slow cooker if necessary. Mix the oil, fennel, garlic chilli, squid, basil stalks, tomatoes and wine in the slow cooker pot. Cover and cook on High for 2–3 hours until the squid and the fennel are tender.

2 Scatter the mussels or clams and the prawns over the sauce, lay the sea bass fillets on top, cover and cook for 30–45 mins more until the mussels or clams have opened and the fish is cooked through and flakes easily. You can keep an eye on the fish through the lid to ensure it doesn't overcook.

3 Serve scattered with the basil leaves and fennel fronds, and eat with crusty bread.

GOOD TO KNOW 2 of 5 a day • low-calorie • healthy • gluten-free
PER SERVING kcals 406 • fat 21g • saturates 4g • carbs 7g • sugars 4g • fibre 3g • protein 43g • salt 0.66g

Turkish lamb pilaf

This is a complete meal in one, with no need for any extra accompaniments, so spoon straight from the pot and tuck in for a casual night in with friends!

TAKES 4½ hours　SERVES 4

- 1 tbsp rapeseed oil
- 2 cinnamon sticks, broken in half
- 1 tsp each ground cumin, coriander and turmeric
- 1 large onion, halved and sliced
- 350g lamb fillet (lean), trimmed of excess fat and cubed
- 250g basmati rice
- 1 lamb or vegetable stock cube
- 8 ready-to-eat dried apricots
- small handful toasted pine nuts or toasted flaked almonds, to serve
- handful mint leaves, roughly chopped, to serve

1 Heat the slow cooker if necessary, then heat the oil in a frying pan. Fry the cinnamon, spices and onion together for 5–10 mins until starting to turn golden. Turn up the heat, stir in the lamb, and fry until the meat changes colour. Tip into the slow cooker pot with the rice and stir to mix.

2 Pour in 500ml boiling water, crumble in the stock cube, add the apricots, then season to taste. Cook on Low for 3–4 hours until the rice is tender and the stock has been absorbed. Toss in the pine nuts or almonds and the mint, and serve.

GOOD TO KNOW 1 of 5 a day • low-cal
PER SERVING kcals 479 • fat 17g • saturates 6g • carbs 55g • sugars 9g • fibre 4g • protein 24g • salt 0.91g

Honey mustard chicken pot with parsnips

For an easy, warming family casserole on a budget, this one-pot ticks all the boxes.

TAKES 4½ hours   SERVES 4

- 1 tbsp olive oil
- 8 bone-in chicken thighs, skin removed
- 2 onions, finely chopped
- 350g parsnips, cut into sticks
- 150ml vegetable stock
- 2 tbsp wholegrain mustard
- 2 tbsp clear honey
- few thyme sprigs
- flat-leaf parsley, to serve (optional)

1 Heat the slow cooker if necessary. Heat half the oil in a large frying pan or shallow casserole with a lid. Brown the chicken until golden, then set aside. Heat the remaining oil, then fry the onions briefly. Tip the onions into the slow cooker.

2 Nestle the thighs amongst the onions and add the parsnips. Mix the stock with the mustard and honey, then pour in. Scatter over the thyme, then cook on Low for 4 hours until the chicken is tender, then season. Serve with parsley leaves and steamed greens.

GOOD TO KNOW healthy • low-salt
PER SERVING kcals 326 • fat 10g • saturates 2g • carbs 23g • sugars 15 g • fibre 6g • protein 39g • salt 0.82g

Succulent braised venison

Venison benefits from long, slow cooking, and this Scottish dish develops a beautifully earthy sweetness – it benefits from being made a day or two ahead and then reheated.

🕐 TAKES 9 hours 🔥 SERVES 8

- 2 carrots, roughly chopped
- 140g turnip or swede, roughly chopped
- 2 onions, roughly chopped
- 3 celery sticks, roughly chopped
- olive oil and butter, for frying
- 1 garlic clove, crushed
- 1kg boned leg or shoulder of venison, cut into large chunks (or buy ready-cubed venison for stewing)
- 5 tbsp plain flour, seasoned with salt and pepper
- 2 tbsp redcurrant jelly (or rowan or hawthorn jelly)
- 100ml dry red wine (Rioja is good)
- 250ml beef stock
- 2 thyme sprigs
- 1 bay leaf

1 Heat the slow cooker if necessary. Fry the vegetables in a little oil and butter in a heavy-based casserole for 4–5 min until golden. Tip in the garlic and fry for a further min, then tip into the slow cooker.

2 Put the venison into a plastic bag with seasoned flour and shake to coat. Add a little more oil and butter to the pan, then fry the venison over a high heat, stirring now and then until well browned. Don't crowd the pan – cook in batches if necessary. Add to the vegetables in the slow cooker.

3 Add the redcurrant jelly and wine to the pan, and bring to the boil, scraping up all the bits that have stuck to the bottom, then pour into the slow cooker. Pour in the stock, then add the thyme and bay leaf. Season if you like and cook on Low for 8 hours. If the sauce is too thin you can pour it off and boil it on the stove to thicken it.

GOOD TO KNOW healthy • low-salt
PER SERVING kcals 277 • fat 10g • saturates 2g • carbs 18g • sugars 2g • fibre 2g • protein 30g • salt 0.7g

Fruity lamb tagine

This tagine benefits from being made in advance and kept for a day or two before being eaten, making it perfect for weekend batch cooking.

 TAKES 8½ hours SERVES 4

- 2 tbsp olive oil
- 500g lean diced lamb
- 1 large onion, roughly chopped
- 2 large carrots, quartered lengthways and cut into chunks
- 2 garlic cloves, finely chopped
- 2 tbsp ras-el-hanout spice mix
- 400g can chopped tomatoes
- 400g can chickpeas, rinsed and drained
- 100g ready-to-eat apricots
- 300ml chicken stock

TO SERVE
- 120g pack pomegranate seeds
- 2 large handfuls coriander, roughly chopped

1 Heat the slow cooker if necessary. Heat the oil in a frying pan and brown the lamb on all sides. Scoop the lamb into the slow cooker, then add the onion and carrots to the pan and cook for 2–3 mins until golden. Add the garlic and cook for 1 min more. Stir in the spices and tomatoes, and season. Tip the lot into the slow cooker with the chickpeas and apricots. Pour over the stock, stir and cook on Low for 6–8 hours.

2 When ready, leave it to rest or transfer to a serving dish so it not piping hot, then serve scattered with pomegranate and herbs, with couscous or rice alongside.

GOOD TO KNOW healthy • low-salt
PER SERVING kcals 497 • fat 18g • saturates 5g • carbs 46g • sugars 32g • fibre 12g • protein 40g • salt 1.37g

Squash, chicken and couscous one-pot

Use up leftovers in this superhealthy one-pot, packed with vital nutrients.

🕐 TAKES 4½ hours 🕐 SERVES 4

- 2 tbsp harissa paste
- 1 tsp each ground cumin and ground coriander
- 2 red onions, halved and cut into thin wedges
- 2 skinless chicken breasts, cut into bite-sized chunks
- 1 small butternut squash, cut into 1cm chunks (no need to peel)
- 2 x 400g cans tomatoes
- zest and juice of 2
- lemons
- 200g cherry tomatoes, halved
- 140g couscous
- small bunch coriander, roughly chopped

1 Heat the slow cooker if necessary. Put the harissa, spices and onions in the pot and mix them together. Add the chicken and and squash, stirring to combine, then tip in th canned tomatoes, cover and cook on Low for 4 hours.
2 Add the lemon zest and juice, cherry tomatoes, couscous and seasoning. Cover and turn off the heat. Leave for 10 mins, then stir through the coriander and serve.

GOOD TO KNOW *healthy • low-salt*
PER SERVING *kcals 283 • fat 3g • saturates 1g • carbs 42g • sugars 16g • fibre 6g • protein 25g • salt 0.53g*

Potroast beef with French onion gravy

Silverside and topside are cheaper and leaner cuts of meat, well-suited to slow-cooking. You'll need a large slow cooker to make this.

 TAKES 11 hours SERVES 4

- 800g-1kg piece silverside or topside of beef that will fit your slow cooker, with no added fat
- 2 tbsp olive oil
- 8 young carrots, tops trimmed (but leave a little, if you like)
- 1 celery stick, finely chopped
- 100ml white wine
- 300ml rich beef stock
- 2 bay leaves
- 500g onions
- a few thyme sprigs
- 1 tsp butter
- 1 tsp light brown or light muscovado sugar
- 2 tsp plain flour

1 Heat the slow cooker if necessary. Rub the meat with 1 tsp of the oil and plenty of seasoning. Heat a large flameproof casserole dish and brown the meat all over for about 10 mins. Meanwhile, add 2 tsp oil to a frying pan and fry the carrots and celery for 10 mins until turning golden.

2 Lift the beef into the slow cooker, splash the wine into the hot casserole and boil for 2 mins. Pour it into the slow cooker with the stock, then tuck in the carrots, celery and bay leaves, trying not to submerge the carrots too much. Cover and cook on High for 1 hour and then Low for 8 hours. If you can, turn the beef once during cooking.

3 During the first hour of cooking, thinly slice the onions. Heat 1 tbsp oil in a pan and stir in the onions, thyme and some seasoning. Cover and cook gently for 20 mins until the onions are softened but not coloured. Remove the lid, turn up the heat, add the butter and sugar, then let the onions caramelise to a dark golden brown, stirring often. Remove the thyme sprigs, stir in the flour, cook for 1 min, then add the onions to the slow cooker.

4 When the beef is ready, it will be tender and easy to pull apart at the edges. Remove it from the cooker and snip off the strings. Slice the beef and bring to the table on a platter, with the carrots to the side and the gravy spooned over.

GOOD TO KNOW healthy • low-salt
PER SERVING kcals 487 • fat 17g • saturates 5g • carbs 19g • sugars 15g • fibre 5g • protein 6g • salt 1g

Pomegranate chicken almond couscous

Jazz up chicken breasts in this fruity, sweetly spiced sauce with pomegranate seeds, toasted almonds and tagine paste. If you avoid dairy, calcium-rich almonds are a good choice to ensure you're getting enough of this bone-building mineral – add a good sprinkle to the top of this.

🕐 TAKES 4½ hours 🥧 SERVES 4

- 1 tbsp vegetable oil
- 1 large red onion, halved and thinly sliced
- 600g chicken mini fillets
- 4 tbsp tagine spice paste or 2 tbsp harissa
- 80ml pomegranate juice (not sweetened)
- ¼ chicken stock cube
- 100g pack pomegranate seeds
- couscous, toasted flaked almonds and chopped mint, to serve

Heat the slow cooker if necessary. Heat the oil in a large frying pan and fry the onion for a few mins to soften it. Scoop into the slow cooker. Brown the chicken briefly in the pan and add to the slow cooker. Stir in the tagine paste or harissa and the pomegranate juice, then crumble in the stock cube and season well. Cook on Low for 4 hours until the chicken is cooked through. Stir through the pomegranate seeds, saving a few to scatter over before serving. Serve the chicken on the couscous with the sauce spooned over and scattered with pomegranate seeds, flaked almonds and the chopped mint.

GOOD TO KNOW healthy
PER SERVING kcals 590 • fat 20 • saturates 2g • carbs 50g • sugars 14g • fibre 4g • protein 50g • salt 0.4g

Smoky beef stew

. . . .

Enjoy this simple stew for dinner, then pack into boxes to keep you going for lunches.

⏱ TAKES 8 hours 🕓 SERVES 6–8

- 1kg stewing beef, cut into large chunks
- 2 onions, chopped
- 2 x 400g cans chopped tomatoes
- 2 tsp each sweet paprika, ground cumin and mild chilli powder
- 1 tbsp red or white wine vinegar
- 2 tbsp golden caster sugar
- 400g can butter beans, rinsed and drained

1 Heat the slow cooker if necessary. Mix the beef, onions, tomatoes, spices, vinegar and sugar in the cooker. Cover and cook on Low for 6–7 hours. Stir in the beans and cook for 30 minutes more or until the beef is tender.

2 Cool any leftovers, then freeze in small food bags or plastic containers. Defrost in microwave or overnight in fridge, then heat in the morning and transfer to a thermos container, or heat in the microwave at lunchtime.

. . . .

GOOD TO KNOW healthy • low-salt
PER SERVING kcals 341 • fat 12g • saturates 5g • carbs 18g • sugars 11g • fibre 4g • protein 42g • salt 0.92g

Braised beef with cranberries and spices

Slow-cook beef with cinnamon, saffron, coriander and harissa for a deeply fragrant rustic casserole.

🕐 TAKES 9–10 hours ◗ SERVES 8

- 2 tbsp olive oil
- 8 thick braising steaks (1kg meat in total)
- 2 large onions, very finely chopped, preferably in a food processor
- 4 garlic cloves, sliced
- 25g ginger, peeled and cut into slivers
- good pinch saffron
- 2 cinnamon sticks, snapped in half
- 1 tbsp ground coriander
- 1 tbsp harissa paste
- 2 tbsp ground almonds
- 600ml hot beef stock
- 2 bay leaves
- 85g dried cranberries

1 Heat a slow cooker if necessary. Heat the oil in a large frying pan. Add the steaks 4 at a time and brown them well on both sides, then transfer to the slow cooker. Now add the onions, garlic and ginger to the oil, plus juices left in the pan, and fry for 5 mins, stirring very frequently. Add the saffron, cinnamon sticks, coriander, harissa and ground almonds and stir well for 1 min, then add to the slow cooker.

2 Tip in the stock, add the bay leaves, cover and cook on Low for 8 hours. Add the cranberries 30 mins before the end of the cooking time so they can plump up in the gravy. Check the beef after the cooking time – it should pull apart easily with 2 forks. If not, cook for another hour. Remove cinnamon and bay leaves.

3 To freeze, cool completely, then pack into freezer bags. Use within 3 months. Thaw in the bags at room temperature for 5–8 hours depending on the bag size, although batches of 2 can be unwrapped and reheated in a pan with a little water in the base. This will also keep in the fridge for a couple of days if you don't want to freeze it. Serve with mash, rice or couscous.

GOOD TO KNOW healthy
PER SERVING kcals 306 • fat 15g • saturates 5g • carbs 15g • sugars 11g • fibre 3g • protein 29g • salt 0.5g

Fragrant spiced chicken with banana sambal

This spicy Asian-inspired dish is flavoured with coriander, cumin, turmeric, almonds and cardamom. Serve with a cooling chopped salad.

🕐 TAKES 4½ hours ⏱ SERVES 6

- 2 large onions, quartered
- 4 garlic cloves
- thumb-sized piece ginger, peeled and roughly chopped
- 300ml low-salt chicken stock
- 1 tsp ground coriander
- 1 tsp ground cumin
- ½ tsp turmeric
- 4 green cardamom pods
- 1 large red chilli, deseeded and finely chopped
- 2 tbsp ground almonds
- 2 tbsp tomato purée
- 500g skinless chicken breasts, cubed
- small pack coriander, chopped

FOR THE SAMBAL AND RICE
(to serve 2, easily doubled)
- 1 small red onion, finely chopped
- ¼ cucumber, peeled, deseeded and diced
- 1 small banana, diced
- zest and juice ½ lime
- 250g pack ready-cooked brown basmati rice, to serve

1 Heat the slow cooker if necessary. Put the onions in a food processor with the garlic and ginger. Blitz until it is as smooth as possible, then pour in half the stock and blitz again. Pour into the slow cooker.
2 Heat a large non-stick pan, sprinkle in the spices and toast for 1 min. Add this to the onion mixture in the slow cooker with the remaining stock and all but ½ tsp of the chopped chilli. Add the almonds and tomato purée, and stir well. Add the chicken and half the fresh coriander. Cook on Low for 4 hours.
3 Mix all the sambal ingredients with the remaining coriander and chilli, and heat the rice following pack instructions. Serve the chicken and sambal with the brown rice.

GOOD TO KNOW healthy • low-fat
PER SERVING kcals 410 • fat 9g • saturates 2g • carbs 48g • sugars 15g • fibre 5g • protein 34g • salt 1.2g

Fish stew with roast garlic and saffron

Try this simpler, lighter version of bouillabaisse, a classic fish soup – serve with toasted slices of baguette to mop up the tomato-based sauce. You can use all kinds of fish for this, depending on what is available. Also the base can be made 3 days ahead or frozen.

 TAKES 6½ hours ⏱ SERVES 6

FOR THE SAFFRON AND GARLIC PASTE

- 3 whole heads garlic
- 150ml good olive oil, plus extra for drizzling
- 50ml Pernod
- good pinch saffron

FOR THE SOUP

- 1 fennel bulb
- 4 celery sticks
- 1 onion
- 1 red chilli, seeds left in
- 2 tbsp olive oil
- 4 garlic cloves
- 2 tbsp fennel seeds
- pinch saffron
- 2 bay leaves
- 50ml Pernod
- 200ml white wine
- 750ml passata
- 3 grey mullet fillets (about 500g in total), skin on, cut into large chunks
- 300g gurnard fillets, skin on, cut into large chunks
- 200g prepared squid and tentacles, cleaned and cut into rings
- juice 1 lemon
- 4 tbsp chopped flat-leaf parsley, plus extra to serve
- toasted slices of baguette, to serve

1 To make the saffron and garlic paste, cut the whole heads of garlic in half horizontally. Place the garlic heads, cut-side up, on a small baking tray. Drizzle over a little olive oil and season with a few good pinches flaky sea salt. Cover with foil and bake for 40–50 mins until softened. Remove the foil and return to the oven for a further 15–20 mins until the garlic has turned golden brown.

2 Pour the Pernod into a small saucepan and add the saffron. Bring to the boil, add the olive oil and warm gently. Take off the heat and leave to cool. Squeeze the cloves out into the bowl of a pestle and mortar. Add a large pinch of flaky sea salt and pound to a paste. Slowly add the saffron-infused olive oil, stirring constantly. Transfer to a clean container and chill until needed.

3 Meanwhile, heat the slow cooker if necessary. Make the soup base. Chop the fennel, celery and onion into small dice and thinly slice the red chilli. Heat the oil in a large frying pan and add the chopped vegetables. Grate the garlic into the pan and add the fennel seeds. Stir well, then cover and fry for 5 mins. Add the saffron and bay leaves, pour in the Pernod and wine, bring to the boil, cook for 2 mins and then tip into the slow cooker. Add the passata. Cook on Low for 4 hours.

4 Transfer the soup to a jug blender and blend until smooth, then pass through a fine sieve, leave to cool and chill in the fridge until needed. The base of the soup can be made 3 days ahead.

5 Bring the soup base to the boil in a large pan, pour back into a heated slow cooker. Add the chunks of prepared fish and squid, and cook on Low for 30 mins. Remove from the heat and stir in the lemon juice and parsley. Ladle the soup into bowls, piling up the fish in the centre. Spoon on the saffron and garlic paste and sprinkle over some more parsley. Serve with toasted slices of baguette and the extra saffron and garlic paste on the side.

GOOD TO KNOW healthy
PER SERVING kcals 345 • fat 13g • saturates 2g • carbs 12g • sugars 9g • fibre 4g • protein 32g
• salt 0.5 g

Lighter cassoulet

This traditionally rich, slow-cooked, French casserole is made healthier with lean gammon steak and pork shoulder for a hearty, warming meal. You can make the base ahead and rehe[c] it to add the sausages if you prefer.

TAKES 5½ hours SERVES 6

- 2 thyme sprigs
- 1 rosemary sprig
- 1 bay leaf
- 1 tbsp rapeseed oil
- 1 medium onion, chopped
- 1 large carrot (200g), chopped into 1cm pieces
- 200g smoked gammon steak, rind and fat removed, cut into lardons
- 2 tsp butter 4 garlic cloves, finely chopped
- 500g pork shoulder, diced into 4-5cm pieces, any excess fat trimmed
- 125ml white wine
- 230g can plum tomatoes
- 1 tbsp tomato purée
- 1 tsp bouillon powder
- 3 Toulouse sausages
- 3 x 400g cans haricot beans in water

FOR THE TOPPING
- 25g panko or coarse dried breadcrumbs
- 1 garlic clove, finely chopped
- 1 tsp finely grated lemon zest
- 2 tsp rapeseed oil

1 Heat the slow cooker if necessary. Wrap the thyme and rosemary sprigs in the bay leaf and tie with string to make [a] bouquet garni. Heat the oil in a large, deep ovenproof sauté pan or frying pan. Put the onion and carrot and lardons in the pan and fry gently on a medium heat for 5 mins, stirring occasionally. Add the butter to the pan, ad[d] the garlic and fry for 2 mins. Increase the heat, add the pork shoulder and fry for 2–3 mins until it is no longer pink. Pour in the wine and let it bubble for 1 min until slightly reduced. Tip everything into the slow cooker. Stir in the tomatoes, tomato purée and bouillon powder, tuck in the bouquet garni, season well with pepper and cook on Low for 3 hours.

2 Meanwhile, heat oven to 180C/160C fan/gas 4. Lay the sausages on a small non-stick baking tray and roast for 20 mins, turning halfway through, until brown. Remove, cut into 1cm-thick diagonal slices.

3 Add the beans to the cassoulet and tuck the sausage slice[s] into the beans, cook on Low for 1-2 hours until bubbling.

4 To serve, mix together the panko crumbs, garlic, lemon zest, oil and some pepper and toast the mixture in a frying pan. By now the meat should be very tender and the cassoulet moist and juicy, not dry. Scatter the crumb mix over.

GOOD TO KNOW healthy
PER SERVING kcals 500 • fat 15.9 • saturates 5.2 • carbs 38.4g • sugars 7.2g • fibre 16.1g • protein 39.7g • salt 1.3g

Mexican pulled chicken and beans

This budget-busting sharing platter of slow-cooked chipotle chicken is perfect for feeding a crowd – try it with the sweetcorn salsa on p270.

 TAKES 7½ hours ◔ SERVES 6–8

- 8 bone-in chicken thighs, skin removed
- 3 tbsp chipotle paste
- 2 garlic cloves, crushed
- 2 x 400g cans chopped tomatoes
- 1 large onion, finely sliced
- 2 x 400g cans black beans, drained
- 400g can kidney beans, drained
- handful parsley, coriander or mint, roughly chopped
- small iceberg lettuce, shredded
- ½ cucumber, diced
- drizzle olive oil
- tortilla chips and lime wedges, to serve

1 Heat the slow cooker if necessary. Rub the chicken thighs with 2 tbsp of the chipotle paste. Put the rest in the slow cooker pot with the garlic, tomatoes, onion and some seasoning. Stir to combine. Sit the chicken thighs close together on top of the sauce. Cover and cook on Low for 6 hours.
2 Add all the beans and stir into the tomato mixture around the chicken. Cook for a further 1 hour.
3 Meanwhile, mix the herbs, lettuce and cucumber with a drizzle of olive oil and set aside.
4 Shred the chicken using a knife and fork, and discard the bones. Mix the chicken through the sauce and beans. Serve with the salad, tortilla chips and lime wedges.

GOOD TO KNOW *healthy • low-fat • gluten-free*
PER SERVING *kcals 251 • fat 6g • saturates 1g • carbs 23g • sugars 8g • fibre 11g • protein 21g • salt 1.2 g*

Cardamom chicken with lime leaves

Slow cookers make excellent curries – the long cooking time allows maximum flavour to be extracted from the spices. Serve with the rice and lentils or use a pack of ready-cooked rice to speed things up.

TAKES 6½ hours | SERVES 4

FOR THE CURRY
- 2 tbsp rapeseed oil
- 1 large onion, finely chopped
- 4 large garlic cloves, grated
- 2 tbsp finely grated ginger
- 12 cardamom pods, seeds removed and lightly crushed
- 4 cloves
- 1 cinnamon stick
- 2 tsp turmeric
- ½ -1 tsp ground white pepper
- 1 tsp ground coriander
- 1 tsp ground cumin
- 1 red chilli, halved, deseeded and finely sliced
- 400g can chopped tomatoes
- 1 tbsp mango chutney
- 2 tsp vegetable bouillon powder
- 1 aubergine, cubed
- 12 boneless, skinless chicken thighs (about 1kg)
- 4 small fresh or dried lime leaves
- 1 green pepper, halved, deseeded and sliced

FOR THE SPICED RICE AND LENTILS
(optional)
- 125g brown basmati rice
- 100g dried red lentils
- 1 tsp cumin seeds
- 1 tsp turmeric
- 1 tsp vegetable bouillon powder

1 Heat the slow cooker if necessary. Heat the oil in a frying pan, add the onion and fry for 5 mins until softened, stirring every now and then. Stir in the garlic, ginger, cardamom, cloves and cinnamon, and cook for 5 mins more, stirring frequently. Add all the remaining spices with the chilli, stir briefly over the heat then add the tomatoes, the chutney and bouillon. Tip the lot into the slow cooker.

2 Stir in the aubergine, chicken and lime leaves. Push them under the liquid and scatter over the green pepper. Cook on Low for 6 hours. Remove the chicken, shred in to medium-sized pieces and return to the sauce.

3 Meanwhile, make the rice. Put all the ingredients in a medium pan with 750ml water. Bring to the boil, then cover and cook for 20 mins. Turn off the heat and leave for 5 mins to absorb any excess moisture. Serve with the curry.

GOOD TO KNOW healthy
PER SERVING kcals 567 • fat 17g • saturates 4g • carbs 49g • sugars 13g • fibre 10g • protein 47g • salt 0.3g

Pork and apple stew with parsley and thyme dumplings

This healthy family supper has dumplings that soak up all the flavours of cider vinegar, mustard and a hint of apple, and it's 3 of your 5-a-day. You can make the base up to 3 days ahead and then reheat it in a casserole and cook the dumplings in the oven at 190C/170C fan/gas 5 for 20-30 minutes.

🕐 TAKES 6¼ hours 🍽 SERVES 4

FOR THE STEW
- 1 tbsp rapeseed oil
- 2 onions, halved and sliced
- 3 celery sticks, thickly sliced
- 2 bay leaves
- 1 tbsp picked thyme leaves
- 500g lean pork fillet, cut into large chunks
- 2 tsp English mustard powder
- 4 large garlic cloves, grated
- 2 tbsp spelt flour
- 2 tbsp cider vinegar
- 400ml bouillon or chicken stock
- 1 Granny Smith apple, peeled, cored and cut into chunks
- 2 leeks, thickly sliced
- 4 carrots, cut into chunks

FOR THE DUMPLINGS
- 140g spelt flour
- 1 tsp baking powder
- 1 tsp English mustard powder
- 2 tbsp finely chopped flat-leaf parsley
- 1 tbsp picked thyme leaves, plus a few sprigs to garnish
- 2 tbsp bio yogurt
- 2 tbsp rapeseed oil

1 Heat the slow cooker if necessary. Heat the oil in a frying pan and add the onions, celery, bay and thyme, and fry for about 8 mins until softened. Add the pork and cook for a few mins until it changes colour, but it doesn't need to brown as you don't want to overcook it.

2 Stir the mustard powder, garlic, flour and vinegar into the frying pan, then pour in the bouillon, stirring to prevent any lumps forming. Tip everything into the slow cooker. Add the apple, leeks and carrots, cover and cook on Low for 5 hours.

3 When the stew is nearly cooked, make the dumplings. Tip the flour, baking powder, mustard powder, parsley and thyme into a bowl and stir to combine. Put the yogurt in a jug, make up to 100ml with water, then stir in the oil. Lightly stir the liquid into the flour to make a soft, slightly sticky dough. Divide the dough equally into eight and shape into balls. Drop them on top of the stew. Cover and cook for a further 1 hour until the dumplings are cooked through. Scatter with the extra thyme, if you like, before serving.

GOOD TO KNOW healthy • 3 of 5 a day
PER SERVING kcals 526 • fat 17g • saturates 3g • carbs 50g • sugars 17g • fibre 13g • protein 36g • salt 0.7 g

Barbacoa beef

This is one of the easiest recipes to cook when you are entertaining. Make a batch of this beef and you can serve it in lettuce cups as shown here, over rice, in tacos or as a topping for salad. If you add plenty of vegetables to whatever you are serving, it will make a healthy meal.

 TAKES 9½ hours SERVES 8–10

- 3 tbsp chipotle paste
- 1 red onion, roughly chopped
- 2 garlic cloves, crushed
- pinch ground cloves
- 2 limes, juiced
- 100ml cider vinegar
- 3 bay leaves
- 500ml low-salt chicken stock
- 1 bunch coriander, roughly chopped
- 1kg brisket, cut into large pieces

TO SERVE
- 2 little gem lettuces, jalapeno chilli slices and half-fat crème fraiche

1 Heat the slow cooker if necessary. Put the chipotle paste, red onion, garlic, cloves, lime juice and cider vinegar into the slow cooker and stir until combined. Add the bay leaves and stock and then put the beef on top. Use a pair of tongs to turn the meat over a few times in the sauce.

2 Put the lid on the slow cooker. Cook on High for 1 hour and then Low for 8 hours or until the meat shreds easily when you pull it apart with 2 forks.

3 Serve with the lettuce cups and jalapeno chillies and crème fraiche.

GOOD TO KNOW healthy
PER SERVING (1 cup) kcals 50 • fat 3g • saturates 1g • carbs 0.5g • sugars 0.4g • fibre 0.3g • protein 4g • salt 0.07g

Pork fillet with apples

Pork and apples are a classic combination and worthy of a dinner party main course. Eating apples will keep their shape even when you cook them for several hours, just make sure you choose ones with plenty of flavour. Serve with 160g peas, 80g courgettes and 80g tenderstem broccoli to make this a complete, healthy meal.

🕐 TAKES 4¼ hours ⏳ SERVES 4

- ½ tbsp rapeseed oil
- 500g pork fillet, sliced into medallions
- 1 medium onion, finely chopped
- 3 eating apples
- 150ml low-salt chicken stock
- 1 tbsp Dijon mustard
- 4 sage leaves, finely sliced
- 2 tbsp half-fat crème fraiche

1 Heat the slow cooker. Heat the oil in a large frying pan, fry the pork medallions in batches on each side for 2 mins until they pick up a little colour. Fry the onion for a few mins, then add the stock and mustard to the pan and stir. Tip the pork and sauce into the slow cooker.

2 Core and cut the apples into quarters, add them to the pot with the sage. Season with black pepper. Cook on Low for 4 hours or until the meat is tender, then stir in the crème fraiche.

GOOD TO KNOW healthy • 2 of 5 a day • low-calorie
PER SERVING kcals 344 • fat 14g • saturates 5g • carbs 18g • sugars 13g • fibre 5g • protein 33g • salt 0.65g

One ingredient chicken

A whole chicken cooks beautifully in a slow cooker, giving a firm flesh with plenty of juices held within it. Eat the chicken as it is or use for one of the other recipes in this book that require cooked chicken such as the spiced black bean soup on p74.

 TAKES 5¼ hours SERVES 6

• 1 large chicken

1 Heat the slow cooker if necessary and add a splash of wat to the base. Scrunch up some foil to make a trivet to sit in th base of the bowl to rest the chicken on. Put the chicken int the pot and season the skin. Cover and cook on Low for 5 hours or until the leg or wing feels very loose when you wiggle it. Tip the juices inside the chicken out as you lift it o

2 Brown the chicken skin under the grill or carve the chicken before anyone sees it. Spoon the liquid out of the base of the pan to use as gravy, there won't be much but it will ha a good flavour.

GOOD TO KNOW gluten-free
PER SERVING kcals 278 • fat 17g • saturates 6g • carbs 0g • sugars 0g • fibre 0g • protein 31g • salt 0.3(

Chapter 5:

VEGAN AND VEGETARIAN SLOW COOKER RECIPES

eans, pulses and so many types of vegetables were made to be slow cooked to perfection. We've got plenty of satisfying, plant-based suppers including a veggie moussaka packed with lentils, aubergine and sweet potato and a smoky aubergine tagine. If you're after comfort food, our potato-topped spiced mushroom and lentil hotpot or vegan shepherd's pie is just the ticket. We've got some veggie classics remade for the slow cooker too – from a vegetable lasagne with wholewheat pasta to an incredibly creamy mushroom risotto that doesn't require hours of stirring at the stove.

Veggie moussaka

This vegetarian version of the classic Greek bake with creamy cheese topping is packed with veg and lentils, making it a good option for a family dinner.

⏱ TAKES 5 hours ◔ SERVES 4–6

- 1 tbsp sunflower oil
- 2 onions, halved and sliced
- 2 garlic cloves, chopped
- 2 bay leaves
- 1 tsp dried oregano
- ½ tsp each ground cinnamon and allspice
- 400g can chopped tomatoes
- 1 tbsp tomato purée
- 140g dried green lentils
- 1 vegetable stock cube
- 200g sweet potatoes, thickly sliced
- 1 large aubergine, sliced and the biggest slices halved again
- 250g low-fat fromage frais
- 1 large egg
- 50g vegetarian feta, crumbled
- 4 tomatoes, thickly sliced

1 Heat the slow cooker if necessary. Heat the oil in a large p◌ and fry the onions and garlic for about 10 mins until golde◌ Stir in the herbs and spices, then tip in the tomatoes and tomato purée, lentils and stock cube with 500ml water. Ad◌ the sweet potato and aubergine, then tip into the slow cooker and cook on Low for 4 hours until the lentils are tender and pulpy. Take off the lid when it is ready to releas◌ any excess steam. Remove the bay leaves.

2 Heat oven to 180C/160C fan/gas 4. Beat the fromage frais◌ egg and cheese together. Tip the lentil mixture into a large ovenproof dish, cover with the cheese mixture, then arrang◌ the tomatoes on top. Grind over some black pepper and bake for 25 mins until the topping is set.

GOOD TO KNOW healthy • 5 of 5 a day • low-calorie • vegetarian • low-fat • high in vitamin C • folate and fibre
PER SERVING kcals 213 • fat 4g • saturates 2g • carbs 30g • sugars 13g • fibre 9g • protein 15g • salt 1g

Giant butter bean stew

This authentic vegetarian casserole makes a delicious first course. Use two cans of tomatoes if you don't have ripe fresh ones.

 TAKES 4½ hours SERVES 6

- 4 x 400g cans butter beans
- 100ml Greek extra virgin olive oil
- 3 small red onions, finely sliced
- 2 large carrots, finely sliced
- 3 celery sticks with leaves, finely chopped
- 4–6 sundried tomatoes, sliced
- 1kg ripe tomatoes, skinned, deseeded and finely chopped
- 4 garlic cloves, chopped
- 1 tsp paprika
- ½–1 tsp ground cinnamon
- 2 tbsp tomato purée
- 1 tsp sugar
- small pack flat-leaf parsley, finely chopped
- small pack dill, finely chopped
- 100g vegetarian feta (optional), crumbled

1 Heat the slow cooker if necessary. Drain the canned beans, reserving the liquid. Heat the oil in a large pan and cook the onions, carrots and celery for a few mins. Stir in the remaining ingredients with 300ml bean juice, reserving half of the chopped herbs and feta, if using.
2 Bring to the boil, tip into the slow cooker, cover and cook on Low for 3–4 hours, stirring once.
3 Stir through the reserved chopped herbs, season to taste, then crumble over the remaining feta just before serving.

GOOD TO KNOW healthy • vegetarian • gluten-free
PER SERVING kcals 315 • fat 18g • saturates 3g • carbs 24g • sugars 12g • fibre 11g • protein 8g • salt 1.1g

224 | Vegan and vegetarian slow cooker recipes

Summer vegetables and chickpeas

This will keep for up to three days in the fridge so you can make it ahead if you like. Vary the colour of the peppers if you usually buy mixed packs.

🕐 TAKES 8¼ hours ◔ SERVES 4

- 3 courgettes, thickly sliced
- 1 aubergine, cut into chunks
- 3 garlic cloves, chopped
- 2 red peppers, deseeded and chopped into chunks
- 2 large baking potatoes, peeled and cut into bite-sized chunks
- 1 onion, chopped
- 1 tbsp coriander seeds
- 4 tbsp olive oil
- 400g can chopped tomatoes
- 400g can chickpeas, drained and rinsed
- small bunch coriander, roughly chopped
- crusty bread, to serve

1 Heat the slow cooker if necessary. Tip all of the vegetables into the slow cooker pot and toss with the coriander seeds, most of the olive oil and some salt and pepper. Pour over the tomatoes and chickpeas, then cover and cook on Low for 6–8 hours until the potatoes are tender.

2 Season to taste, drizzle with the remaining olive oil, then scatter over the coriander. Serve from the pot or pile into a serving dish. Eat with hunks of crusty bread.

GOOD TO KNOW healthy • vegan • low-salt
PER SERVING kcals 327 • fat 15g • saturates 2g • carbs 40g • sugars 13g • fibre 9g • protein 11g • salt 0.51

Smoky aubergine tagine with lemon and apricots

This fragrant tagine is perfect for summer entertaining, packed with satisfying meaty aubergines and aromatic spices. It's worth frying the aubergine properly first to give them a melting, tender texture.

TAKES 2½ hours   SERVES 4

- 2 aubergines, cut into large chunks
- 3 tbsp olive oil
- 2 onions, chopped
- 2 tbsp freshly grated ginger
- 1½ tsp each ras el hanout and smoked sweet paprika
- good pinch saffron
- 300ml hot vegetable stock
- 1 preserved lemon, chopped (optional)
- 120g ready-to-eat dried apricots, halved
- 200g tomatoes, roughly chopped
- 1 tbsp clear honey
- juice 1 lemon
- zest 1 lemon or ¼ preserved lemon, finely sliced
- 2 tsp toasted sesame seeds
- 2 tbsp each finely chopped flat-leaf parsley and mint
- Greek yogurt, to serve (optional)
- wholemeal bulghar wheat, to serve (optional)

1 Heat the slow cooker if necessary. Brown the aubergines in 2 tbsp of the oil so they're golden on all sides, but not soft in the middle yet – this is best done in batches in a large, non-stick frying pan. Tip them into the slow cooker.

2 Add the remaining oil to the frying pan, then add the onions, ginger and spices and fry gently until softened and golden. Tip into the slow cooker.

3 Meanwhile, add the saffron to the stock to soak. Stir the preserved lemon, if using, apricots, tomatoes, honey and lemon juice into the veg in the slow cooker with the saffron stock. Cook on High for 2 hours until the aubergines are tender. Season to taste.

4 Mix the lemon zest, sesame seeds and chopped herbs together, and sprinkle over the tagine. Serve with Greek yogurt and wholegrain bulghar wheat, if you like.

GOOD TO KNOW healthy • vegetarian
PER SERVING kcals 327 • fat 15g • saturates 2g • carbs 40g • sugars 13g • fibre 9g • protein 11g • salt 0.5g

Tomato and chilli harissa

Make your own spice paste to use in marinades, Moroccan tagines, dips and soups. It will keep for several months and is endlessly useful. The heat of your harissa will depend entirely on how hot your chillies are.

TAKES 5 hours MAKES 1 x 350g jar

- 1 tsp each caraway seeds and coriander seeds
- ½ tsp cumin seeds
- 100ml olive oil, plus a little extra
- 4 garlic cloves, peeled but kept whole
- 1 tsp smoked paprika
- 500g tomatoes, deseeded and chopped
- 3 red chillies, deseeded (use more chillies and leave the seeds in if you like it very fiery)
- 1 tsp rose water (optional)

Heat the spice seeds in a dry pan until lightly toasted and aromatic then lightly crush using a pestle and mortar. Heat the slow cooker if necessary. Mix the oil, garlic, toasted spices, paprika, tomatoes and chillies in the pot. Cover and cook on High for 2 hours until the tomatoes are softened and pulpy. Remove the lid and cook for 1–2 hours more, stirring occasionally, until tender and thickened. Remove from the heat, add the rose water, if using, then blitz with a stick blender or pulse in a food processor to make a rough paste. Spoon into a sterilised jar and pour a little oil on the surface to cover it completely. Will keep in the fridge for several months if you cover the surface with oil after each use.

GOOD TO KNOW healthy • vegan
PER SERVING kcals 34 • fat 3g • saturates 1g • carbs 1g • sugars 1g • fibre 0g • protein 0g • salt 0g

Red lentil squash dhal

A hearty budget meal of spiced red lentils with butternut and tomatoes. Add coriander, cumin, turmeric and a dollop of mango chutney for a flavour boost.

TAKES 5¼ hours   SERVES 4

- 1 tbsp sunflower oil
- 1 onion, finely chopped
- 1 garlic clove, finely chopped
- 1 tsp ground coriander
- 1 tsp ground cumin
- 1 tsp turmeric
- ½ tsp cayenne pepper
- 400g butternut squash, peeled and cut into 2cm chunks (prepared weight)
- 400g can chopped tomatoes
- 600ml vegetable stock, boiling
- 1 heaped tbsp mango chutney
- 300g red lentils
- small pack coriander, roughly chopped
- naan bread, to serve

1 Heat the slow cooker if necessary. Put the oil and the onion in a frying pan, and cook for 5 mins. Stir in the garlic and cook for a further 1 min, then stir in the spices and butternut squash. Combine everything together and tip into the slow cooker.

2 Tip in the chopped tomatoes, stock and chutney, and season well. Add the lentils and cook on Low for 5 hours until the lentils and squash are tender. Sprinkle on the coriander and serve with warmed naan bread.

GOOD TO KNOW *healthy • vegetarian • low-fat*
PER SERVING *kcals 485 • fat 12g • saturates 2g • carbs 58g • sugars 14g • fibre 9g • protein 42g • salt 0.6g*

Chunky butternut mulligatawny

Halfway between a soup and a stew, this low-fat and low-calorie recipe is perfect for batch cooking.

⏱ TAKES 4½ hours ◔ SERVES 6

- 2 tbsp olive or rapeseed oil
- 2 onions, finely chopped
- 2 dessert apples, peeled and finely chopped
- 3 celery sticks, finely chopped
- ½ small butternut squash, peeled, seeds removed, chopped into small pieces
- 2–3 heaped tbsp gluten-free curry powder (depending on how spicy you like it)
- 1 tbsp ground cinnamon
- 1 tbsp nigella seeds (also called black onion or kalonji seeds)
- 2 x 400g cans chopped tomatoes
- 400–600ml gluten-free vegetable stock , brought to a boil
- 140g basmati rice
- small pack parsley, chopped
- 3 tbsp mango chutney, plus a little to serve, (optional)
- natural yogurt, to serve

1 Heat the slow cooker if necessary. Heat the oil in a frying pan and fry the onions, apples and celery. Add the butternut squash, curry powder, cinnamon, nigella seeds and a grind of black pepper. Cook for 2 mins more, then tip into the slow cooker and stir in the tomatoes, stock and rice. Cook on Low for 4 hours.

2 By now the vegetables should be tender but not mushy and the rice cooked. Taste and add more seasoning if needed. Stir through the parsley and mango chutney, then serve in bowls with yogurt and extra mango chutney on top, if you like.

GOOD TO KNOW healthy • vegetarian • gluten-free
PER SERVING kcals 212 • fat 5g • saturates 1g • carbs 37g • sugars 15g • fibre 6g • protein 6g • salt 0.5g

Vegetable tagine with almond and chickpea couscous

Batch cook this during the weekend and you'll only have to reheat this and make the couscous on a weeknight.

🕐 TAKES 4¾ hours ◔ SERVES 4

- 400g pack shallots, peeled and cut in half
- 2 tbsp olive oil
- 1 large butternut squash, about 1¼kg, peeled, deseeded and cut into bite-sized chunks
- 1 tsp ground cinnamon
- ½ tsp ground ginger
- 450ml strong-flavoured vegetable stock
- 12 small pitted prunes
- 2 tsp clear honey
- 2 red peppers, deseeded and cut into chunks
- 3 tbsp chopped coriander
- 2 tbsp chopped mint, plus extra for spinkling

FOR THE COUSCOUS
- 250g couscous
- 1 tbsp harissa paste
- 400g can chickpeas, rinsed and drained
- handful toasted flaked almonds

1 Heat the slow cooker if necessary. Fry the shallots in the oil for 5 mins until they are softening and browned. Add the squash and spices, and stir for 1 min. Pour in the stock, season well, then add the prunes and honey, bring to a boil and carefully tip into the slow cooker.

2 Add the peppers and cook on Low for 4 hours until just tender. Stir in the coriander and mint.

3 Pour 400ml boiling water over the couscous in a bowl, then stir in the harissa with ½ tsp salt. Tip in the chickpeas, then cover and leave for 5 mins. Fluff up with a fork and serve with the tagine, flaked almonds and extra mint.

GOOD TO KNOW healthy • vegetarian • 1 of 5 a day • high in fibre • folate and iron
PER SERVING kcals 483 • fat 11g • saturates 1g • carbs 85g • sugars 33g • fibre 10g • protein 15g • salt 0.61g

Pea and new potato curry

If you use fresh peas for this you can make your own stock by cooking leftover pea pods in water with mint, thyme and parsley for 35 mins.

⏱ TAKES 2½ hours ◔ SERVES 4

- 1 tbsp vegetable oil
- 2 onions, sliced
- 3 red chillies, deseeded and finely sliced
- thumb-sized piece ginger, roughly chopped
- 2 tsp cumin seed
- 1 tsp Madras curry powder
- ½ tsp turmeric
- 750g new potatoes, halved
- juice 1 lime
- small bunch coriander, stalks and leaves finely chopped
- 100ml vegetable stock, or pea stock (see intro)
- 300g podded fresh peas (or use frozen)
- 250ml pot natural yogurt
- lime wedges, to serve
- 2 naan breads, to serve

1 Heat the slow cooker if necessary. Heat the oil in a large, deep frying pan. Add the onions and cook over a low heat for 10–15 mins until soft. Throw in the chillies, ginger and spices, and cook for a few mins. Stir in the potatoes and lime juice, coating in the spice mix. Tip everything into the slow cooker.

2 Add the coriander stalks and the stock. Cook on Low for 2 hours until the potatoes are soft, stir through the peas and cook for another 30 mins. Cool a little. Stir in the yogurt, a little at a time so it doesn't curdle. Sprinkle over the coriander leaves, and serve with lime wedges and warm naan bread.

GOOD TO KNOW healthy • vegetarian
PER SERVING kcals 336 • fat 8g • saturates 3g • carbs 50g • sugars 18g • fibre 9g • protein 16g • salt 0.5g

Spinach sweet potato and lentil dhal

A comforting vegan one-pot recipe that counts for 3 of our 5-a-day! You can't go wrong with this iron-rich, low-fat, low-calorie supper.

⏱ TAKES 4½ hours ◔ SERVES 4

- 1 tbsp sesame oil
- 1 red onion, finely chopped
- 1 garlic clove, crushed
- thumb-sized piece ginger, peeled and finely chopped
- 1 red chilli, finely chopped
- 1½ tsp turmeric
- 1½ tsp ground cumin
- 2 sweet potatoes (about 400g), cut into even chunks
- 250g red split lentils
- 300ml vegetable stock
- 80g bag spinach
- 4 spring onions, sliced on the diagonal, to serve
- ½ small pack Thai basil, leaves torn, to serve

1 Heat the slow cooker if necessary. Heat the oil in a frying pan. Add the onion and cook over a low heat for 10 mins, stirring occasionally, until softened. Add the garlic, ginger and chilli, cook for 1 min, then add the spices and cook for 1 min more. Tip everything into the slow cooker.

2 Add the sweet potato and stir everything together so the potato is coated in the spice mixture. Tip in the lentils, stock and some seasoning, cover and cook on Low for 4 hours until the lentils are tender and the potato is just holding its shape

3 Taste and adjust the seasoning, then gently stir in the spinach. Top with the spring onions and basil to serve. Or allow to cool completely, then divide between airtight containers and store in the fridge for a healthy lunchbox.

GOOD TO KNOW healthy • vegetarian • low-fat
PER SERVING kcals 397 • fat 5g • saturates 1g • carbs 65g • sugars 19g • fibre 11g • protein 18g • salt 0.6g

Moroccan vegetable stew

This stew is packed with nourishing ingredients like fibre-full chickpeas and iron-rich lentils.

⏱ TAKES 4½ hours ⏲ SERVES 4

- 1 tbsp cold-pressed rapeseed oil
- 1 medium onion, peeled and finely sliced
- 2 thin leeks, trimmed and cut into thick slices
- 2 large garlic cloves, peeled and finely sliced
- 2 tsp ground coriander
- 2 tsp ground cumin
- ½ tsp dried chilli flakes
- ¼ tsp ground cinnamon
- 400g can chopped tomatoes
- 1 red pepper, deseeded and cut into chunks
- 1 yellow pepper, deseeded and cut into chunks
- 400g can chickpeas, drained and rinsed
- 100g dried split red lentils
- 375g sweet potatoes, peeled and cut into chunks
- juice 1 large orange plus 1 strip of zest made with a vegetable peeler
- 50g mixed nuts, such as brazils, hazelnuts, pecans and walnuts, toasted and roughly chopped
- ½ small pack coriander, roughly chopped, to serve
- full-fat natural bio-yogurt, to serve (optional)

1 Heat the slow cooker if necessary. Heat the oil in a large flameproof casserole or saucepan and gently fry the onion and leeks for 10–15 mins until well softened, stirring occasionally. Add the garlic and cook for 2 mins more.

2 Stir in the ground coriander, cumin, chilli and cinnamon. Cook for 2 mins, stirring occasionally. Season with plenty of ground black pepper. Tip everything into the slow cooker. Add the chopped tomatoes, peppers, chickpeas, lentils, sweet potatoes, orange zest and juice, half the nuts and 100ml water and bring to a simmer. Cook on Low for 4 hours, until the potatoes are softened but not breaking apart.

3 Ladle the stew into bowls. Scatter with coriander and the remaining nuts and top with yogurt, if using.

GOOD TO KNOW healthy • vegetarian • gluten-free
PER SERVING kcals 482 • fat 14g • saturates 2g • carbs 63g • sugars 26g • fibre 15g • protein 18g • salt 0.6g

Mushroom stifado

Red wine, mushrooms, baby onions, herbs and spices make this a satisfying stew to serve with rice or mash.

🕐 TAKES 7¼ hours 🕐 SERVES 4

- 25g dried porcini mushrooms
- 2 tbsp olive oil, plus extra for drizzling
- 500g pickling onions
- 1kg mixed mushrooms such as oyster, cep, chestnut, morel, Portobello
- 3 garlic cloves, finely chopped
- 125ml dry red wine
- 1 tbsp tomato purée
- 2 tbsp red wine vinegar
- 2 bay leaves
- 5 whole allspice berries
- 1 large or 2 small cinnamon sticks
- 4 whole cloves
- 1 tsp black peppercorns
- 2 tomatoes, peeled and finely chopped
- 75g Kalamata black olives, pitted and chopped
- 2 tsp Greek clear honey
- 3 tbsp chopped flat-leaf parsley
- 50g vegetarian kefalotyri/ pecorino, grated (optional)

1 Heat the slow cooker if necessary. Soak the dried porcini in 100ml boiling water for 30 minutes. Heat half the oil in a large frying pan. Add the whole onions and a splash of water, and cook over a low heat until caramelised, about 20 mins, stirring occasionally. Tip the onions into the slow cooker.

2 Meanwhile, cut the fresh mushrooms into halves and quarters, to give rough 4cm pieces. Once the onions have been removed from the pan, add the remaining oil and cook the fresh mushrooms and garlic over a medium heat for 10 mins until browned, stirring frequently. Pour in the wine and cook for 5–10 mins until reduced by half, add to the slow cooker.

3 Tip the porcini and soaking liquid into the slow cooker with the tomato purée, vinegar, bay leaves, allspice, cinnamon, cloves, peppercorns and tomatoes. Cook on Low for 6 hours. Add the olives and honey, and season to taste. Sprinkle with the parsley and cheese.

GOOD TO KNOW healthy • vegetarian • gluten-free
PER SERVING kcals 419 • fat 29g • saturates 4g • carbs 19g • sugars 14g • fibre 9g • protein 11g • salt 1.4g

Kidney bean curry

Cheap, delicious and filling, this curry can be endlessly embellished – try stirring in spinach at the end. This will keep for up to three days, can be easily reheated and makes a good lunchbox leftover.

 TAKES 4¼ hours SERVES 2

- 1 tbsp vegetable oil
- 1 onion, finely chopped
- 2 garlic cloves, finely chopped
- thumb-sized piece ginger, peeled and finely chopped
- 1 small pack coriander, stalks finely chopped, leaves roughly shredded
- 1 tsp ground cumin
- 1 tsp ground paprika
- 2 tsp garam masala
- 400g can chopped tomatoes
- 400g can kidney beans, drained
- cooked basmati rice, to serve

1 Heat the slow cooker if necessary. Heat the oil in a large frying pan over a low-medium heat. Add the onion and a pinch of salt and cook slowly, stirring occasionally, until softened and just starting to colour. Add the garlic, ginger and coriander stalks and cook for a further 2 mins, until fragrant. Add the spices to the pan and cook for another 1 min, by which point everything should smell aromatic. Tip in the chopped tomatoes and kidney beans, then bring to the boil. Tip everything into the slow cooker.

2 Cook on Low for 4 hours until the curry is aromatic. Season to taste, then serve with the basmati rice and the coriander leaves.

GOOD TO KNOW healthy • vegan • gluten-free
PER SERVING kcals 282 • fat 8g • saturates 1g • carbs 33g • sugars 13g • fibre 14g • protein 13g • salt 0.1g

Double bean roasted pepper chilli

This warming vegetarian chilli is a low-fat, healthy option that packs in the veggies and flavour. Leftovers can be eaten on toast or as a filling for baked potatoes. You will need a large slow cooker for this, or simply halve the recipe.

 TAKES 5½ hours, SERVES 8

- 2 onions, chopped
- 2 celery sticks, finely chopped
- 2 yellow or orange peppers, finely chopped
- 2 tbsp sunflower oil or rapeseed oil
- 2 x 460g jars roasted red peppers
- 2 tsp chipotle paste
- 1 tbsp red wine vinegar
- 1 tbsp cocoa powder
- 1 tbsp dried oregano
- 1 tbsp sweet smoked paprika
- 2 tbsp ground cumin
- 1 tsp ground cinnamon
- 2 x 400g cans chopped tomatoes
- 400g can refried beans
- 3 x 400g cans kidney beans, drained and rinsed
- 2 x 400g cans black beans, drained and rinsed

1 Heat the slow cooker. Put the onions, celery and chopped peppers with the oil in your largest frying pan, and fry gently over a low heat until soft but not coloured.

2 Drain both jars of peppers. Put a quarter of the peppers into a food processor with the chipotle paste, vinegar, cocoa, dried spices and herbs. Whizz to a purée, then stir into the softened veg and cook for a few mins. Tip everything into the slow cooker.

3 Add the tomatoes and refried beans. Cook on Low for 4 hours until smoky and the tomato chunks have broken down to a smoother sauce.

4 At this stage you can cool and chill the sauce if making ahead. Otherwise add the kidney and black beans, and the remaining roasted peppers, cut into bite-sized pieces, then cook for a further 1 hour. (This makes a large batch, once the sauce is ready you can freeze half and only add half the amount of beans to make a smaller finished batch). Once the beans are hot, season to taste and serve

GOOD TO KNOW healthy • vegetarian • gluten-free
PER SERVING kcals 327 • fat 6g • saturates 1g • carbs 41g • sugars 9g • fibre 18g • protein 19g • salt 0.6g

Spiced mushroom lentil hotpot

A vegan winter warmer the whole family will love – this healthy potato-topped bake is low in calories and fat, high in fibre and 3 of your 5-a-day.

TAKES 5 hours   SERVES 4

- 2 tbsp olive oil
- 1 medium onion, sliced
- 300g mini Portobello mushrooms or chestnut mushrooms, sliced
- 2 garlic cloves, crushed
- 1½ tsp ground cumin
- 1 tsp smoked paprika
- 2 x 400g cans green lentils, drained and rinsed (drained weight 240g)
- 1 tbsp soy sauce
- 1 tbsp balsamic vinegar
- 1 medium sweet potato, peeled and very thinly sliced
- 1 large potato, very thinly sliced
- 1 thyme sprig, leaves picked

1 Heat the slow cooker if necessary. Heat half the oil in a medium saucepan. Fry the onion until soft, then add the mushrooms. Cook until the mushrooms are nicely browne then increase the heat and add the garlic, ground cumir and paprika, and cook for 1 min. Remove from the heat and add the lentils, soy sauce and balsamic vinegar. Season, then tip the mixture into the slow cooker.

2 Rinse the saucepan and return to the hob. Add a kettle fu of boiled water and bring back to the boil over a high he Add the potato slices, cook for 3 mins, then drain. Arrang on top of the lentils. Cook on Low for 4 hours until the potatoes are tender. Preheat the grill. Brush the remaining oil over the potato and grill the top then scatter over the thyme before serving.

GOOD TO KNOW *healthy • vegan • low-fat*
PER SERVING kcals 312 • fat 7g • saturates 1g • carbs 44g • sugars 13g • fibre 12g • protein 12g • salt 0.7g

Cauliflower, olive and lentil tagine

Packed with veg, this provides an amazing 4 of your 5-a-day. You can swap the black olives f
green if you prefer, or leave them out.

TAKES 5 hours • SERVES 4

- 1 tbsp rapeseed oil
- 1 large onion, finely chopped
- 2 garlic cloves, finely chopped
- 1 tbsp chilli powder
- 1 tsp ground cumin
- 2 tsp ground coriander
- 400g can chopped tomatoes
- ½ lemon, zest grated
- 2 tbsp tomato purée
- 12 black olives, halved
- 1 tbsp vegetable bouillon powder
- 4 large carrots, cut into batons
- 1 small cauliflower, cut into florets
- 400g can green lentils, drained
- ⅓ small pack fresh coriander, chopped
- 200g bulghar wheat

1 Heat the slow cooker if necessary. Heat the oil in a large frying pan, add the onion and garlic and stir-fry briefly to soften them a little. Add the spices, then pour in the tomatoes and stir in the lemon zest, tomato purée, olives and bouillon powder. Tip into the slow cooker. Add the carrots and cauliflower to the pan then cover and cook Low for 4 hours until they are tender. Stir in the lentils and most of the coriander and cook for a further 30 minutes.

2 While the tagine is cooking, cook the bulghar following pack instructions. Serve the tagine sprinked with the remaing coriander and the bulghar.

GOOD TO KNOW healthy • vegetarian • low-fat
PER SERVING kcals 336 • fat 7g • saturates 1g • carbs 46g • sugars 16g • fibre 17g • protein 13g • salt 0.8

Vegan shepherd's pie

A warming vegan supper that's low calorie, low fat and perfect for when the nights draw in. The base and potatoes will keep for up to 3 days in the fridge so you can make them ahead and finish the dish on the day you want to eat it.

🕐 TAKES 4 hours 🕐 SERVES 8

- 1.2kg floury potatoes, such as Maris Piper or King Edward, cut into chunks
- 50ml vegetable oil
- 30g dried porcini mushrooms, soaked in hot water for 15 mins, then drained (reserve the liquid)
- 2 large leeks, chopped
- 2 small onions, chopped
- 4 medium carrots (about 300g), cut into small cubes
- 1 vegetable stock cube
- 3 garlic cloves, crushed
- 2 tbsp tomato purée
- 2 tsp smoked paprika
- 1 small butternut squash, peeled and cut into small cubes
- ½ small pack marjoram or oregano, leaves picked and roughly chopped
- ½ small pack thyme, leaves picked
- ½ small pack sage, leaves picked and roughly chopped
- 4 celery sticks, chopped
- 400g can chickpeas
- 300g frozen peas
- 300g frozen spinach
- 20ml olive oil
- small pack flat-leaf parsley, chopped
- tomato ketchup, to serve (optional)

1 Put the potatoes in a large saucepan, cover with water, bring to the boil and simmer for 20 mins or until tender. Drain and leave cool a little.

2 Meanwhile, heat the slow cooker if necessary. Heat the vegetable oil in a large heavy-based sauté pan or flameproof casserole dish. Add the mushrooms, leeks, onions, carrots and stock cube and cook gently for 5 mins, stirring every so often. If starts to stick, reduce the heat and stir more frequently, scraping the bits from the bottom. The veg should be soft but not mushy.

3 Add the garlic, tomato purée, paprika, squash and herbs. Stir and turn the heat up a bit, cook for 3 mins, add the celery, then stir and cook for a few more mins. Scrape everything into the slow cooker.

4 Tip in the chickpeas and reserved mushroom stock. Add the peas and spinach and stir well. There should still be plenty of liquid and the veg should be bright and a little firm.

5 Mash 200g of the potato with a fork and stir into the veg. Break the rest of the potatoes into chunks, mix with the olive oil and parsley and season, set aside.

6 Cook on Low for 3 hours. Divide the mixture among smaller dish and top with the reserved potato. Preheat the grill and grill the top of the pies to turn the top of the potato golden to serve. Se with tomato ketchup, if you like.

GOOD TO KNOW healthy • vegan • low-fat • low-calorie
PER SERVING kcals 348 • fat 11g • saturates 1g • carbs 43g • sugars 10g • fibre 13g • protein 11g • salt 0.5g

Lentil ragu with courgetti

A healthy tomato 'pasta' dish that makes full use of your spiralizer. This vegan-friendly supper is 5 of your 5-a-day. If you don't have a spiraliser then most supermarkets sell ready prepared courgetti.

🕐 TAKES 2½ hours 🕐 SERVES 4–6

- 2 tbsp rapeseed oil, plus 1 tsp
- 3 celery sticks, chopped
- 2 carrots, chopped
- 4 garlic cloves, chopped
- 2 onions, finely chopped
- 140g button mushrooms from a 280g pack, quartered
- 500g pack dried red lentils
- 500g pack passata
- 500ml low-salt vegetable bouillon
- 1 tsp dried oregano
- 2 tbsp balsamic vinegar
- 1–2 large courgettes, cut into noodles with a spiraliser, julienne peeler or knife

1 Heat the slow cooker if necessary. Heat the 2 tbsp oil in a large sauté pan. Add the celery, carrots, garlic and onion and fry for 4–5 mins over a high heat to soften and start to colour. Add the mushrooms and fry for 2 mins more. Stir in the lentils, passata, bouillon, oregano and balsamic vinegar and bring to a boil. Tip into the slow cooker. Cover and cook on Low for 2 hours until the lentils are tender and pulpy.

2 To serve, heat the remaining oil in a separate frying pan, add the courgette and stir-fry briefly to soften and warm through. Serve half the ragu with the courgetti and chill the rest to eat on another day. Can be frozen for up to 3 months.

GOOD TO KNOW healthy • vegan • gluten-free
PER SERVING kcals 578 • fat 7g • saturates 1g • carbs 87g • sugars 19g • fibre 14g • protein 35g • salt 0.2g

Gigantes plaki

Satisfying and superhealthy, enjoy at room temperature as part of a meze, or on top of toasted sourdough.

TAKES 5¼ hours SERVES 4

- 400g dried butter beans or 2 x 400g cans
- 3 tbsp Greek extra virgin olive oil, plus more to serve
- 1 Spanish onion, finely chopped
- 2 garlic cloves, finely chopped
- 2 tbsp tomato purée
- 800g ripe tomatoes, skins removed, roughly chopped
- 1 tsp golden caster sugar
- 1 tsp dried oregano
- pinch ground cinnamon
- 2 tbsp chopped flat-leaf parsley, plus extra to serve

1 If using dried beans soak them overnight in plenty of water. Drain, rinse, then place in a pan covered with water. Bring to the boil, reduce the heat, then simmer for approx 50 mins until slightly tender but not soft. Drain, then set aside.

2 Heat the slow cooker if necessary. Heat the olive oil in a large frying pan, tip in the onion and garlic, then cook over a medium heat for 10 mins until softened but not browned. Add the tomato purée, cook for a further min, add remaining ingredients, then simmer for 2–3 mins. Season generously, then stir in the beans (the canned beans go in now too). Tip into the slow cooker, then cook on Low for 4 hours. The beans will absorb all the fabulous flavours. Tip into a serving dish, allow to cool a little, then scatter with parsley and drizzle with a little more olive oil to serve.

GOOD TO KNOW healthy • vegan
PER SERVING kcals 431 • fat 11g • saturates 1g • carbs 66g • sugars 15g • fibre 19g • protein 22g • salt 0.2g

Mushroom risotto

* *

Contrary to belief, risotto doesn't need constant stirring. This creamy risotto made in a slow cooker will surprise you.

 TAKES 1½ hours SERVES 4

- 1 onion, finely chopped
- 1 tsp olive oil
- 250g chestnut mushrooms, sliced
- 800ml vegetable stock
- 50g porcini
- 300g wholegrain rice
- small bunch parsley, finely chopped
- grated vegetarian Parmesan-style cheese to serve

1 Heat the slow cooker if necessary. Fry the onion in the oil in a frying pan with a splash or water for 10 minutes or until it is soft but not coloured. Add the mushroom slices and stir them around until they start to soften and give off their juices.

2 Meanwhile pour the stock into a saucepan and add the porcini, bring to a simmer and then leave to soak. Tip the onions and mushrooms into the slow cooker and add the rice, stir it in well. Pour over the stock and porcini leaving any bits of sediment in the saucepan (or pour the mixture through a fine sieve).

3 Cook on High for 1 hour and then check the consistency, the rice should be cooked. If it needs a little more liquid stir in a splash of stock. Stir in the parsley and season. Serve with the Parmesan.

* *

GOOD TO KNOW 1 of 5 a day • low-fat • low-calorie • vegetarian • healthy
PER SERVING kcals 346 • fat 3g • saturates 0.3g • carbs 67g • sugars 5g • fibre 5g • protein 10g • salt 0.5

Vegetable lasagne

This is perfect for days when you want to go meat free. The layers are based on ratatouille, which packs in plenty towards your 5-a-day.

TAKES 3½ hours • SERVES 4

- 1 tbsp rapeseed oil
- 2 onions, sliced
- 2 large garlic cloves, chopped
- 2 large courgettes, diced (400g)
- 1 red and 1 yellow pepper, deseeded and roughly sliced
- 1 large aubergine, sliced
- 400g can chopped tomatoes
- 2 tbsp tomato purée
- 2 tsp vegetable bouillon
- 15g fresh basil, chopped plus a few leaves
- 6 wholewheat lasagne sheets (105g)
- 125g vegetarian buffalo mozzarella, chopped

1 Heat the oil in a large non-stick pan and fry the onions and garlic for 5mins, stirring frequently until softened. Tip in the courgettes, peppers, aubergine and tomatoes with the tomato purée, bouillon and chopped basil. Stir well, cover and cook for 5 mins. Don't be tempted to add any more liquid as plenty of moisture will come from the veg once they start cooking.

2 Put 4 slices of aubergine in the base of the slow cooker and top with 2 sheets of lasagne. Add a third of the ratatouille mixture, then 2 more lasagne sheets, then the remaining lasagne and veg mix. Cover and cook on High for 2½-3 hours until the pasta and vegetables are tender. Turn off the machine.

3 Scatter the mozzarella over the vegetables then cover and leave for 10 mins to settle and melt the cheese. Scatter with basil and serve with a handful of rocket.

GOOD TO KNOW healthy • vegetarian . • 5 of 5 a day • low-calorie • low-fat • high in vitamin C • folate and fibre
PER SERVING kcals 325 • fat 11g • saturates 5g • carbs 36g • sugars 17g • fibre 11g • protein 15g • salt 0.44g

Chapter 6

SALADS AND SIDES

· ·

Slow cookers are an absolute godsend in the kitchen but the one thing you can't make in them is fresh salad or salsa. So in order to give you a selection of perky, green sides and super-fresh accompaniments we've added a chapter of quick recipes such as crunchy radish and tomato salad, avocado panzanella and sweetcorn salsa to serve with your slow cooker favourites.

Radish, lentil and mint salad

Frequently underrated, radishes are bright and crunchy in any salad. Look out for all the wonderful varieties such as daikon radishes and especially red meat radishes, which look li a greenish/white turnip but hides a surprising hot-pink middle.

⏱ TAKES 45 mins 🥧 SERVES 4

FOR THE RELISH
- 50g walnut pieces,
- 3 tbsp olive oil
- 1 red onion, sliced
- 1 tsp black treacle
- 2 tbsp sherry vinegar
- small pack mint, leaves picked and half chopped
- 400g can green lentils, drained and rinsed
- 1/2 cucumber, chopped
- 300g radishes, some left whole, others sliced and chopped

1 Toast the walnut pieces in a large frying pan over a medium heat until fragrant and just starting to char at edges. Tip into a bowl and set aside.

2 In the same pan, turn the heat down to low and add 1 olive oil. Add the onion, fry gently for around 10 mins u soft, then take the pan off the heat. Add the black trec Sherry vinegar and the rest of the olive oil, then mix an leave to cool. Add the chopped mint to the pan, and season well.

3 In a large bowl, mix together the lentils, cucumber anc the radishes, then pour over the cooled onion and min dressing. Toss everything together and pile onto a servi dish. Scatter over the walnut pieces and the rest of the and radishes, then serve.

GOOD TO KNOW gluten-free • healthy
PER SERVING kcals 244 • fat 17g • saturates 2g • carbs 14g • sugars 7g • fibre 4g • protein 6g • salt 0.1g

Avocado panzanella

Use up any stale, leftover bread in this bright side salad with avocado, red onion and ripe tomatoes. Try it with our low-fat turkey Bolognese (p140) or our classic lasagne (p162).

🕐 TAKES 20 mins 🥧 SERVES 4

- 800g mix of ripe tomatoes
- 1 garlic clove, crushed
- 1½ tbsp capers, drained and rinsed
- 1 ripe avocado, stoned, peeled and chopped
- 1 small red onion, very thinly sliced
- 175g ciabatta or crusty loaf
- 4 tbsp extra virgin olive oil
- 2 tbsp red wine vinegar
- small handful basil leaves

1 Halve or roughly chop the tomatoes (depending on size) and put them in a bowl. Season well and add the garlic, capers, avocado and onion, and mix well. Set aside for 10 mins.

2 Meanwhile, tear or slice the ciabatta into 3cm chunks and place in a large serving bowl or on a platter. Drizzle with half the olive oil, half the vinegar and add some seasoning. When ready to serve, pour over the tomatoes and any juices. Scatter with the basil leaves and drizzle over the remaining oil and vinegar. Give it a final stir and serve immediately.

GOOD TO KNOW Healthy • Vegan
PER SERVING kcals 332 • fat 21g • saturates 4g • carbs 30g • sugars 8g • fibre 6g • protein 7g • salt 0.9g

Sweetcorn salsa

Sweet, crunchy corn pairs perfectly with jalapeno, coriander, lime and feta to make an accompaniment bursting with flavour. Try it with our turkey chilli with jacket potatoes (p148) or our Mexican pulled chicken and beans (p212).

TAKES 20 mins SERVES 4

- 4 fresh corn cobs
- 2 vine tomatoes, chopped
- ½ red onion, chopped
- 1 red pepper, deseeded and chopped
- 1 avocado, stoned, peeled and chopped
- 1 jalapeno pepper, deseeded and finely chopped
- handful coriander, roughly chopped
- juice 3 limes
- 75g feta

1 Boil the corn for about 5 mins or until tender. Run under cold water and drain thoroughly. Cut the corn off the cob and put in a large serving bowl.
2 Add the tomatoes, onion, red pepper, avocado, jalapeno pepper, coriander, lime juice and seasoning, and mix well. Crumble over the feta to serve.

GOOD TO KNOW healthy • gluten-free • vegetarian
PER SERVING kcals 227 • fat 13g • saturates 4g • carbs 20g • sugars 7g • fibre 4g • protein 8g • salt 0.7g

Middle Eastern carrot salad

The texture of this crunchy shredded carrot makes a great contrast to tender, slow-cooked dishes, and the flavours of fragrant orange blossom water, cumin and mint make it special enough for entertaining. Try it with our smoky aubergine tagine with lemon and apricots (p232).

PREP 15 mins no cook · SERVES 4

- ½ tsp orange blossom water
- ½ tsp ground cumin
- 1 tbsp extra virgin olive oil
- juice ½ lemon
- 500g carrots, shredded or grated
- large handful small mint leaves

1 Put the orange blossom water, cumin, oil, lemon juice and some seasoning into a jar. Screw on the lid and shake well to combine.
2 Tip the carrots and mint into a bowl. Pour over the dressing, season and toss everything together.

GOOD TO KNOW healthy · gluten-free · vegan
PER SERVING kcals 69 · fat 3g · saturates 1g · carbs 9g · sugars 9g · fibre 4g · protein 1g · salt 0.1g

Peppery fennel and carrot salad

Thinly sliced, crisp veggies combine with crunchy nuts and a punchy dressing in this recipe, perfect with Indian spiced dishes. Try with our red lentil squash dhal (p236).

TAKES 10 mins   SERVES 6

- 2 large carrots, cut into thin sticks or grated
- 2 large fennel bulbs, quartered and thinly sliced
- handful peanut or cashew nuts, chopped
- 2 tbsp olive oil
- 1 tsp mustard seeds
- 1 tsp nigella or black onion seeds (optional)
- juice 1 lemon or lime

Tip the carrots and fennel into a salad bowl. Toast the nuts in a hot frying pan for 3–5 mins until golden, then tip onto a plate. In the same pan, heat the oil and fry the mustard and nigella or black onion seeds, if using, until they begin to pop – about 30 secs. Pour in the lemon or lime juice and mix together to make a dressing. Toss together with the vegetables in the bowl, then sprinkle with nuts to serve.

GOOD TO KNOW *vegetarian* • *healthy*
PER SERVING *kcals 87 • fat 6g • saturates 1g • carbs 6g • sugars 5g • fibre 3g • protein 2g • salt 0.05g*

274 | Salads and sides

Roasted squash and red onion with pistachios

A vibrant vegan side salad with roasted butternut squash, jewel-like pomegranate seeds and crunchy pistachios. Try alongside our chicken and chickpea tagine (p142).

🕐 TAKES 40 mins   🕐 SERVES 4

- 1 large butternut squash, peeled, ends trimmed, halved widthways and spiralised into thick noodles
- 1 large red onion, peeled, ends trimmed and spiralised using the ribbon attachment
- 2 tbsp olive oil
- 2 tsp sumac
- 50g pomegranate seeds
- 30g pistachios, toasted and roughly chopped

1 Heat oven to 200C/180C fan/gas 6. Toss the spiralised butternut squash and onion together with the oil, sumac, some sea salt and black pepper in a roasting tray. Spread out then roast for 25 mins until the vegetables are completely tender and beginning to caramelize.

2 Divide among plates and top with the pomegranate seeds and toasted pistachios.

GOOD TO KNOW healthy • gluten-free • vegan
PER SERVING kcals 197 • fat 9g • saturates 1g • carbs 21g • sugars 13g • fibre 6g • protein 4g • salt 0g

Runner beans with rocket and Parmesan

This light green salad with walnuts and tangy Italian cheese makes a great addition to Mediterranean meals. Try it with our classic lasagne (p162).

TAKES 15 mins COOK 5 mins   SERVES 4

- 50ml extra virgin olive oil
- juice 1 lemon
- 300g runner beans, stringed and sliced
- 50g walnut halves, roughly chopped
- 50g bag wild rocket
- 25g Parmesan (or vegetarian alternative) shavings

1 Mix the olive oil with the lemon juice, season and set aside. Boil a large pan of salted water, then cook the beans for about 8 mins until tender. Drain well and leave to cool a little.
2 Toss the beans with half the dressing, the walnuts and rocket. Place in a serving dish and scatter with the Parmesan, then drizzle over the remaining dressing.

GOOD TO KNOW healthy • vegetarian
PER SERVING kcals 242 • fat 23g • saturates 4g • carbs 3g • sugars 2g • fibre 3g • protein 5g • salt 0.3g

Lemony three bean and feta salad

A fresh, low-calorie salad crammed with green, edamame and cannellini beans. Try it with our veggie moussaka (p226).

🕐 TAKES 20 mins 📤 SERVES 4

- 200g green beans, trimmed and halved lengthways
- 200g frozen soya or edamame beans
- 400g can cannellini beans, drained and rinsed
- ½ red onion, finely chopped
- juice 1 lemon
- pinch caster sugar
- 1 tsp poppy seeds
- 85g feta, crumbled

Cook the green beans and edamame beans together in a pan of boiling water for 3 mins until tender. Drain and cool under cold running water, then drain again and mix with the cannellini beans and red onion. Add the lemon juice, sugar, poppy seeds and seasoning and stir through. Scatter the feta on top, then divide among plates.

GOOD TO KNOW vegetarian • healthy
PER SERVING kcals 318 • fat 12g • saturates 5g • carbs 31g • sugars 7g • fibre 7g • protein 23g • salt 1.7g

Index

GET OUR
AWARD-WINNING DIGITAL MAGAZINE

+ EASY-TO-VIEW RECIPE MODE

DOWNLOAD NOW